The TAMING of the CREW

Working Successfully with Difficult Students

Brian D. Mendler

Teacher Learning Center is proud to provide their educational expertise in the areas of classroom management, student motivation, and discipline to school districts all over the world. Drs. Allen Mendler, Richard Curwin, and Brian Mendler, co-authors of the best selling book, *(Discipline with Dignity 3rd edition: New Challenges New Solutions,)* and their associates offer a variety of consulting and training programs emphasizing practial, reasearch based strategies that can be immediately implemented in the classroom. Our lively, fast paced seminars offer cutting-edge information in an entertaining and engaging way.

Contact:
Discipline Associates, LLC
dba Teacher Learning Center
PO Box 20481
Rochester, NY 14602
Phone: 800-772-5227
Fax: 585-292-5545
Info@tlc-sems.com
www.tlc-sems.com

To contact Brian Mendler for keynote, on-site training, institutes, and webinars, call 800-772-5227.

Printed in the United States of America.
Design by Blue Water Printing

ISBN 978-0-578-03081-4

Dedication

To my brother, Dr. Jason Mendler: Your tireless effort to make this world a better place for those with cancer is inspiring. You continue to teach me so much about work ethic, dedication, patience, perseverance, and loyalty. I love you.

To my sister, Lisa: You are 14 years younger than me and somehow I learn from you every day. I am so proud of the beautiful young woman you have become. I smile when I watch you work with little kids. You have a gift with them that I hope you take full advantage of in your life. You will be amazing at whatever you choose to do. I love you.

Acknowledgements

A special thanks to all of my students both past and present, for allowing me the opportunity to make a difference in your lives. I am your teacher, but fortunately I continue to learn as much from you as you do from me. I feel truly blessed.

To my father, friend, colleague, partner, and co-author, Allen Mendler. Thanks so much for the outstanding editing you did on this book. Words cannot describe how much I appreciate your mentoring, guidance, support, and patience. I love you.

To my mom for doing the final edits on this book, and of course for your constant love, support, and guidance. Thanks for everything. I love you.

Jason, Ticia, Caleb, Ava, and my soon to be niece: I love you very much. I am so proud to have such an amazing family.

To my beautiful sister Lisa, I am so proud of you. It was a pleasure watching you grow up into a wonderful, kind, compassionate, young woman. I love you so much.

To my grandmother, Nancy Klein, thanks for your support, love, and guidance.

To Jon Crabbe at the Teacher Learning Center for believing in me. I have learned so much about the business side of education from you. Your organization skills, dedication, friendship, support, guidance and perspective are qualities I continue to count on every day. Thanks for helping make this book and my consulting career a reality. I could not have done it without you.

Thanks to Rick Curwin, my colleague, co-author, and friend, for helping guide my career. You are an amazing teacher and workshop presenter. I continue to learn from you.

To Allison for 15 years and Susan for 2 years of loyal service to Discipline Associates and the Teacher Learning Center. Thanks for believing in me.

To our outstanding team of associates that continue to use and present our work: Jerry Evanski, Willeta Corbett, Colleen and Dave Zawadzki, and Mary Beth Hewitt. You are the best.

To all the people at Corwin Press and ASCD for doing a great job publishing my first two books. I appreciate the opportunities your organizations have helped create for me.

To Kerry Macko, my friend and co-teacher at St. John Fisher College, thanks for the never ending stream of strategies you provide our students and me. I am fortunate to share many of these with educators all over the world.

To Mr. Bill Dalton: A dedicated English Teacher that inspired me to change my behavior. Thank you for being the teacher that never quit on me. I will remember you always.

To some of my favorite and most influential teachers, administrators, and colleagues: The world is a better place because of you. Thanks for all you do on a daily basis to make the lives of our students better and to help push my work forward.

- Jim Decamp, (English Teacher), Rush-Henrietta High School

- Pat Woityra (English Teacher), Wheatland-Chili High School

- Marcus Hartel (Resource Room), Penfield High School

- Linda Steinberg (5th Grade Teacher), Fyle Elementary School

- Becky Zelesnikar (4th Grade Teacher), Longridge Elementary School

- Renee Marion, (Math Teacher), Hillsides Halpern Education Center

- Laura Milanette, (Spanish Teacher), Wheatland-Chili High School

- Kimbe Lange (Principal), Kyle Elementary School

- Mary Hawk (Principal), Meigs Middle School

- Doug Curnes (Kindergarten teacher), Kyle Elementary School

- Tracy Vik (Staff Development Coordinator), Sioux Falls Public Schools

Table of Contents

Introduction

A short woman with jet black hair, a very tan face, and a ton of energy came up to me at a seminar in Orlando after lunch and said, "I have to tell you something that just happened in my room to see how you would have handled it. I mean, I think I said the right thing, but I want your opinion. This 8th grade boy said he wasn't going to take out his homework. He said I couldn't make him do anything. Then he looked at me and in front of the whole class he said, 'you motherfu**er.' Brian, there was dead silence in the room. They all wanted to see and hear what I was going to do next. So I looked directly into his eyes and with a stern, almost nasty tone I replied, 'You got it half right. But I don't have any children yet!' He was stunned. The class laughed, and the situation was diffused."

It reminded me of Bethany. She was a challenging 17 year old junior I worked with a few years back. In the middle of class she raised her hand and said this: "Mr. Mendler, you're a giraffe looking asshole." It takes a lot to surprise me, but I think the fact that she raised her hand to insult me is what did it. Instinctively I looked at my paraprofessional and said, "Do you think I look like a giraffe?" She shrugged and said, "Well, you do have a long neck and a big nose." I glared at Bethany and said, "You know, next time you want to tell me I look like a giraffe can it at least wait until after the lesson? And by the way, you called me an asshole. But admit I'm cool sometimes too. Go on, admit it. I'm a cool asshole." Bethany had a totally confused look on her face. She said, "Of course you're cool sometimes." I was so happy.

Early in my career an administrator told me the best teachers are the "coolest assholes" you've ever met. If you're always cool, students will walk all over you. If you're always an asshole they will hate you. So you better be both.

Bethany ended up graduating from high school. Two years later my cell phone rang. It was a number I did not recognize. "Mr. Mendler? It's Bethany. Remember me?" Of course I did. "I need to thank you." I asked, "For what?" Then she said what no student said before her and no one has said since. "Thank you for being tougher in not giving up on me than I was in trying to get you to quit. I tried everything Mr. Mendler. I was rude and nasty. I called you names. I insulted you. I told you I hated you. But you never stopped caring about me. You never stopped pushing me. You never gave up on me despite my best efforts to get you to. So thanks Mr. Mendler. Take care." She hung up. I have not heard from her since. I write this book for Bethany and for all of your Bethany's. In it, I provide hundreds of specific strategies, and overall principles that allow me to reiterate what Bethany said, "be tougher in not giving up on my students than they are in trying to get me to quit." Enjoy.

CHAPTER ONE

It Is All About Relationships

S trong student/teacher relationships are vital to any well run classroom. Have you ever heard a teacher say, "I'm not here for him to like me, I'm here for him to learn." I agree. But isn't it easier getting someone to learn when they like you? There are three major times we can build relationships with our students:

1. **In class** when they are supposed to be there and we are teaching our content.

2. **In school** but outside of our class.

3. **Outside of school**.

Each will be addressed in this chapter and specific relationship building strategies within each category will be shared.

In-Classroom Relationship Building:

In my opinion this is the hardest. How is it possible to build individual relationships with students when we are supposed to be teaching the entire group? It takes a lot of skill and a willingness to incorporate relationship building into the curriculum. Wise teachers realize that they will ultimately save lots of time since kids who like

---

and respect their teacher are far less likely to disrupt their class.

Hammer, Hammer, Hammer, Hug?

When needing to correct a student's behavior, the "four H's" are the way to go. Each "hammer" is a correction or criticism directed at a student. Each "hug" is compliment or praise. It is very important that when you have to "hammer" you balance it with a "hug." Here is an example:

Mr. M. (1st Hammer): Walking into class late is not ok.

(2nd Hammer): I am extremely disappointed in you for disrupting on your way in.

(3rd Hammer): You and I are going to come up with a consequence so this does not happen again. We will do it right after class.

(Hug): By the way, that is a really cool outfit you have on. Where did you get it?

The "hug" part is so important because it allows us to "hammer" again tomorrow! If we only approach students to "hammer" their guard goes up. We become predictable and students prepare an excuse. But if we "hug" every once in a while the guard stays down and the hammers actually find their target. By the way, it is not always necessary to "hammer" three times. Use your judgment.

Use PEP (Privacy, Eye Contact, Proximity) when talking to a Student:

We have written about this strategy many times before (Mendler, Curwin, & Mendler 2008). Both praise and correction should be done as privately as possible. Publicly praising often annoys and aggravates the other students. Publicly correcting usually prompts a defensive response. When using PEP try hard to get as close to the student as possible, make direct eye contact, and deliver a message quickly and directly. In some schools and cultures the eye contact piece is not important and might backfire. Focus on privacy and proximity. As soon as the message is spoken, get out of there. Do not stick around for a response. Say what you need to say and move. When used effectively a teacher can compliment and correct a student within a few minutes of each other. Be sure to tell the class that during the year you will often be delivering messages that are only for individual ears and you will not be delivering that message to the entire group. This keeps students from wondering what the private message was you delivered.

At times I define this as a *"hit and run."* Speak quick, direct, firm, and then move right into something else. The movement part is so important to making this work. I will refer to the "movement" part of this many more times throughout this book.

Keep Hands in Pockets:

At seminars I am often accused of "touching my butt." I do not realize I am doing it, but I did learn it is a defense mechanism related to PEP. I am so used to delivering individual messages in extremely close proximity that I naturally put my hands in my pockets. This accomplishes two things. First it ensures I do not make physical contact with a student. Second, when people get animated and upset their hands tend to flail.

By keeping them in, the movement looks controlled.

Proper Position to Greet Students:
We all know that it is good practice to greet our students at the door as they arrive. However, one of my former principals taught me the best way to position myself to remain in control at all times. Stand straight up at the door with your arms folded across your chest.

Keep one foot in the room and the other in the hallway. Try to smile. In this position we can do three things at once without moving. We can say good morning to a student walking in, turn our head one way to tell those in the room to get to work, and the other way to see what is going on in the hall. The arms crossed position is one of authority. By smiling we show we are inviting and in charge at the same time. If all staff in the building is positioned this way almost nothing is missed!

Don't be afraid to make time for student issues!
When teaching in a block schedule (usually 60-80 minutes), this becomes easier. Take 10 minutes every day to talk with and listen to your students. Let them know they will have time to talk with each other. You can also use it for individual conversations. Tell your class there will be times you will just sit and listen to their conversations. Be very clear that after 10 minutes the lesson will start. I prefer the first 10 minutes because usually my students want to talk to each other

during this time anyway. Then I can listen to what they are talking about and teach a lesson based on something someone says. This usually happens within the first 5-7 minutes. So I really end up giving only 5 minutes of talk time if I am prepared to take over the lesson by using their talk as a segue to the content. There are times I use the first 10 minutes to lead a discussion about an issue I know is relevant to them or to teach a life skill that they will need. I recall Carol, telling me that I "have no idea what it is like to go home to paid employees every day. I don't have a mom and a dad. I live in a group home. So whatever with your stupid English assignment." Needless to say, this warrants a few minutes of my time. Here are a few discussion topics for building relationships:

- Discuss bullying and role-play bullying situations.
- Teach and role-play how to get along with teachers they do not like (Do not allow them to use names).
- Conduct practice job interviews. Students can pair up one being the employer and one being the person seeking the job.
- Discuss what a "goal" is and how to reach it.
- Have a student write one thing they will do today to help reach that goal.
- Allow class clowns to tell jokes or be the center of attention (for a predetermined amount of time).
- Teach students to dress professionally: The difference between business casual, formal, informal, etc...

- Tell them one thing you are struggling with in life (i.e. an issue regarding child-rearing since kids love to be the "expert" in this field) and then ask for advice.

If teaching in a shorter period, giving this time is more difficult. Cutting from 10 to 5 minutes each day is one option. I still prefer 10 every other day if there is not time.

If you have a class all day (usually elementary or self-contained), try picking a block of time. I like at least 20 minutes. With younger kids the discussion should be more focused. The above bullet points are good topics. Unfortunately, most state curriculums do not build this in. Make time anyway. These are the conversations that allow us to learn about our students. I know it sounds cliché, but remember, students will only care to learn when they first learn that we care.

Find the Leaders:

Some teachers tell me their entire class is out of control. They ask what to do when everyone is constantly disrupting. Find the leaders. The goal is to figure out who they are. Work hard at getting them on your side since they often have the leverage to influence everyone else. Realize that we usually need them more than they need us. The leaders already have everyone else. Most classes have 2-3 leaders. It should not take long to figure out who they are. In most classes it will be obvious. If you are not sure who they are, here are some things to look for:

- After giving a request, who does everyone look at?
- In elementary schools who do they want to sit by at lunch?

- In middle and high schools who are the good athletes?
- Which students seem popular?
- Who is not afraid to yell "shut up" to the entire class and usually gets others to quickly comply?

Get them Started:

One of the best ways to have an individual conversation in a group setting is to get the rest of the class started on a project, test, quiz, or homework assignment. As they work independently, wander over to the student you need to speak with. This is a great time to ask a private question or to find out more about his or her life. The key is that now there are a few minutes to get it done while others are focused on something else. Be sure to have a few group activities in your back pocket in case there is a pressing need to deal with an individual issue.

2x10:

My father and Dr. Curwin first came up with this strategy in their best-selling book, *Discipline with Dignity* (1988). The "2" stands for two consecutive minutes, the "10" stands for ten consecutive days. The goal is to begin developing a relationship with a student that rarely participates. Here are the steps that make it work.

1. Get the rest of your class started on something else.
2. Approach the student from the side.
3. Get down to his or her level (or slightly below).

4. Begin the conversation in as quiet and calm a voice as possible.

Below is the 2x10 in action: My eyes are wandering the room as I am talking to Tony as he probably is not looking at me:

Mr. M: Hey Tony. I see your head is down. Are you tired?

Tony: (No response)

Mr. M: (after pausing which is important to teach Tony it is his turn to talk) Sometimes I am tired when I'm in school. And I get paid to be here! If you could be anywhere else in the world right now where would it be?

Tony: (shrugging his shoulders) Home.

Mr. M: Really? How come? Do you enjoy being home? What's your favorite thing to do at home?

This dialogue lasts for two minutes. Notice Tony does not respond to the initial question of "are you tired?" The pause shows him it is his turn to respond. When he does not I answer my own question. If nothing else he is going to learn about me. Relationships are a two way street. Many teachers believe students should tell us about them but we don't have to reciprocate. Sometimes I end up having a conversation with myself. Get used to it. In reality almost always the student will respond after a few questions. Try learning what sport he likes, what his home life is like, what his interests outside of school are. If he does not respond tell him your favorite sport, etc... With this knowledge it is easier to work with him in the future. Be sure to get your other students started on something so they are not paying attention to the conversation. In this activity it is not important to make eye contact. Many kids like him will not look at us anyway. They usually have their heads down.

When first attempting this, look at a clock for a start and end time. Remember, only two minutes. Trust me, it is long enough. With certain students that are extremely difficult to converse with you might try a one minute intervention until becoming comfortable with this strategy. To watch me demonstrate this, visit www.tlc-sems.com.

Get Out of my Face:

Once in a while a student will tell me to get out of his or her face. I always do. But as I am walking away I usually say, "Ok. But I will be back to talk to you again later."

What do I do when the others want to know what we talked about?

Great question, and at first some students will wonder what you said to Tony. Be sure to say the following phrase to your entire class at the beginning of the year (or as soon thereafter as you can). "Hey guys, I need to let you know a few things about how this year is going to work in here (or if later in the year "a few changes we are going to make.") There are going to be times this year that I have private, individual conversations with different people in this class. Sometimes it will be to correct a behavior, other times to praise something you are doing well. Occasionally it will be just to chat with you about life. I just want to let you know that when this happens I will not be sharing what was said with anyone else. The conversation will remain between that student and me. Trust me; I will drop by your desk to talk to you just as often as I do your neighbor. Sound good?" After a few reminders they quickly learn this is how our classroom works.

Helping Hands for a Great Community:
    The Helping Hands strategy is best done in lower grades although it works for older kids as well. Students trace one of their hands on a piece of paper. Each hand is then cut out and placed on a bulletin board titled, "I feel safe when" and "I learn best when." Each student writes an answer to the phrase on their cutout hand and each is posted on a bulletin board or wall in the classroom. The teacher can refer back to the hands when struggling to figure out different student learning styles, etc... This is another solid relationship building strategy.

Outside of Class but Still In-School Relationship Building:
    This might be the single most important tool in the relationship building box. It is critical that we get to know our students outside of the normal, scheduled time required to be with them. Here are a few places inside of school but outside of class we can find them to build relationships. They are ranked from my favorite to least favorite. I'll explain why below.

- Hallways in between classes (middle and high school).
- Student Cafeteria (all grades).
- Recess (elementary).
- Bus loop when students are entering and leaving (all grades).
- Gym (all grades).
- Art Room (all grades).
- Music Room (all grades).

Connect in Noisy Places:

Remember this rule: It is almost always beneficial to utilize the loudest, most chaotic places in the school to build relationships since these actually offer the most privacy. The noise makes it near impossible for anyone else to hear.

Hallways:

For middle and high school teachers there is no better place to understand and see school dynamics in action. Positioning yourself in the hallway in between classes is an important behavior management tool. Your presence matters! While watching you will almost always see leaders quickly emerge. Some may be in your class. Some might not. Either way, make it a priority to get to know all students. Hallways are places for the masses. They are often noisy with students going in all different directions. The noise and mass movement make it a perfect place for a private conversation. It is easy to pull a student aside amid the chaos to compliment her outfit, new hair style, or to ask a personal question. I love to ask a quick question in the hallway and then follow up by telling the student if they want to talk more, this is when I'm available. Make a commitment to doing this at least one time every day. If you have a class and can not be in the hallway, try to position yourself at the door in the manner described earlier.

Student Cafeteria:

The student cafeteria often looks chaotic. But remember, loud conversations and students paying attention to each other are a perfect recipe for private conversation amid the chaos. Sometimes just stand at a distance and observe class dynamics. There is a lot to learn just by watching. Usually when observing I prefer they not see me. However, many times I will approach a student and ask him to walk with me for a second or two. Be sure to start the conversation by reminding him that it is your lunch right now and you are taking your lunch to talk with him. For example, "Johnny, right now I could be doing a lot of other things, but I am really concerned about you. In fact, I chose to give up my lunch to try figuring out what is going on. Can you please fill me in?" When kids see I am willing to work with them on my own time they immediately garner a higher level of respect. The student cafeteria can also be a great place to meet students you do not have in class. The lunch monitors and cafeteria crews will really like it when you spend time in the student cafeteria. Finally, when cafeteria staff see us trying to connect with difficult students, it gives them a bit of a break. More than once, I have earned some "brownie points" in the form of a free chocolate chip cookie!

Recess:
Here is a list of activities to do with students during recess. Remember, there is a difference between doing and watching.

- Baseball/softball catch
- Shoot hoops
- Jump rope
- Hop scotch
- Double Dutch
- Races
- Swings

- Hula Hoop
- Video Games
- Dance Revolution
- Checkers or chess

Try to get started in a game or activity with them. After a few minutes let someone fill in so you can have a one-on-one chat with a student or small group. After the chat get right back to the activity. You might even have a private sign-up sheet available for students that want to talk with you. Be sure to set time limits as some students are so needy they will dominate your every moment!

Bus Loop:

Get out by the buses in the morning and greet students as they get off. Then stand outside near the bus loop when they leave. This is a place to have a quick conversation about whatever. You will remind some about homework, wish others good luck in their game, or tell someone else you will be thinking about them since things at home are not going well right now. The bus loop is one of my favorite places to position myself for relationship building. It won't hurt your standing in the eyes of most administrators either.

The Gym or Another Teacher's room:

The gym is my favorite because the combination of loud noise and mass controlled chaos is usually present. Plus, I love sports. Just ask the teacher if you can have two minutes with a particular student. I have never had a problem. If there is absolutely no other time to connect and a compelling reason to see the student more immediately, ask a colleague to either send the student to see you or to allow you a few minutes with the student in his class.

Outside of the School Relationship Building:
Some of the best relationship building is done when students see us outside of school. It is hard for me to understand teachers that refuse to live in the town they teach because they might "run into students." What's wrong with that? Let them see you in a hooded sweatshirt, jeans, and a hat on backwards. It shows there is a time and place to dress a certain way. One of my students works at my dry cleaner, two at a restaurant I frequent, and one where I get my car washed. I hope they are working when I am there. This gives me a conversation starter for the next day at school.

Attend games, plays, recitals, and anything else that can fit into your busy life outside of school. These events help tremendously and if you have time to attend everything, do it. But if not, here is the secret to making it look like you are at everything while actually going to very little.

It is More Important to be Seen than to See:
Sometimes I go to a basketball game, wrestling meet, school play etc... and can not or do not want to stay the whole time. The secret is to get there a few minutes before the event begins. Find your student and make sure he or she sees you. Make eye contact, wave, or if you can, personally greet him. I can't tell you how many basketball games I was at for warm-ups. When the ball was tossed I was out of there. It is important for me to see my student but more importantly he needs to see me! The next day I can talk to him about the game

and how he did. Just be sure to ask the coach what the final score was and a few things about the game. Showing up at the end is ok too. Again, be sure not to leave until you are positive the student has seen you.

This is especially good for newer teachers not yet tenured. Usually there is an administrator at every school event. Be sure they see you. Make eye contact, wave, or personally greet them. Then when they are not looking, duck out. Your administrators will think you are amazing, and that you attend *every* event! I'll never forget a letter of recommendation a former principal wrote for me that said, "Brian is at everything. He is ultra-involved in their lives, especially outside of school. I don't know how he does it!" Now she knows.

A few other relationship building techniques to use outside of school:

- Have students volunteer with you.
- Ask them to attend your events outside of school (I play softball and golf).
- Go to their house to say hello or see how they are doing. Just get parental permission and be sure another adult is always home. Stopping by to see a student that is sick, suspended, or a constant disruption can go a long way in getting them to comply upon return.

Invite them over?

Are there a hundred reasons not to invite a student over? Yes. But a well conceived invite in a proper social situation can be an exceptionally meaningful moment in the life of a child as well as an effective behavior management strategy. Carol did not have parents. She lived in a group home and was always miserable around holiday time. As Thanksgiving was around the corner, I remember talking to my mom about her, feeling sad that Carol had nobody special with whom to share the holiday. My mom, who was a teacher, suggested inviting her for thanksgiving dinner with my family. Arrangements were made for a case manager from the group home to drive her, stay for dinner, and then bring her home. There were about 20 people at my house that night. Carol sat next to my mom. She was perfectly well behaved. She even helped clean up the dishes. Carol never disrupted my class again.

He is suspended and I can build a relationship?

You bet. Most of the time teachers call home and tell parents what their child is doing wrong. This is important and needs to be done. But here is a relationship building phone call my friend and colleague Kerry Smith had with a student that was just suspended. She called home the night he left school. The conversation went like this:

Ms. S: Hey Chris, It is Ms. Smith. I heard you were suspended for three days. I'm really sorry it happened and I am just calling to tell you I'll miss you when you're gone.

Chris: But I didn't even do...

Ms. S. (cutting him off): You know what? I wish I had time to hear the whole story right now but unfortunately I don't. I just want to tell you I look forward to you coming back. I hate when you are suspended. I know you rarely get any work done when gone, but if for some crazy reason you decide not to fall even farther behind, I can bring some assignments to work on. If not, that's fine too. Listen, if you feel angry and start thinking about doing something that might get you into more trouble, feel free to give me a call first. I am always here to listen. Again, sorry you're gone. Please try to stay out of trouble. I will see you in a few days.

Most teachers suspend a student with the message: "Good Riddance." Even when feeling that way, try hard not to show it. Very few teachers make this call. Be the one that does. It takes about 30 seconds and gets about a month of good behavior when the student returns. I try calling suspended students every night during the suspension to ask how they are as well as to offer a reminder about what they can do that is school-related while home.

Relationship Building Phrases:

Here are a few of my favorites. You can fill in the blanks.

- I'm really proud of how you did (fill in the blank).
- I saw your (fill in the blank). I really liked it.
- When I was your age I did that too... So don't worry. But here is what you can do instead.
- I like your (fill in the blank). Where did you get it?
- Did you know they all like to follow you? You're a great leader.
- Since everyone follows you anyway, can you please help me (fill in the blank).

Calling to correct almost always starts with something positive!

When calling a parent to correct be sure to start with something positive. Look for an adjective that describes the student in a decent way. Here is an example of a phone call Ms. Cunneyworth made to Anna's mother:

Ms. C.: Hi Mrs. Anna. This is Ms. C. I teach Anna every day 4th period. How are you?

Mrs. A: I'm not sure.

Ms. C: I want you to know that Anna is one of the most **determined** people I have ever taught. And overall, that is a good thing. Anna is also a **tremendous leader** and has the ability to easily influence others. They follow her, listen to her, and often do what she says. Again, these are all qualities I really like about her. Unfortunately sometimes she leads them in a negative way. Anna could be a major force in this class helping to prevent bullying. Lately I feel like she has been influencing others to pick on Karen who is new to our class. I think with your help we can get her going in the right direction.

Mrs. A: Well what can I do about it?

Ms. C: You can start by commending Anna on her leadership skills. Tell her I called and told you how many good qualities she has. Explain to her that it is important that she lead her friends in a positive way. You might even tell her that you (her mom) were sometimes picked on in school and that it made you feel awful. Tell her that you wished there was someone like Anna in your class that was courageous enough to help get it to stop. Then ask her if any bullying goes on in her class. She will probably say no and then ask you if I said she was a bully. Tell her that I said sometimes I think she can utilize those leadership skills in a better way, but overall I am really proud of her. Then ask if you can count on her to help stop any bullying that she sees.

Mrs. A: Ok, sounds good. I'll talk with her.

Let's analyze this conversation. Ms. C. picked the word "determined" to describe Anna. Ms. C. told her mom that Anna is a great leader and has no problem getting others to follow her. These are qualities Ms. C. truly likes. Now mom is much more likely to listen to suggestions because Ms. C. praised her daughter first. She mentions that it seems like Anna is influencing others in a negative way, and then gives a specific example (Karen). Notice how it is phrased in a non-threatening way. Ms. C. never says Anna is a bully. Instead, she is "influencing" others to pick on Karen. Next Ms. C. tells Anna's mom that she thinks "we" can help get it to stop. This gets her to ask what she can do to help. Remember, many parents have no idea what they can do. We need to offer specific suggestions. Ms. C. then asks Anna's mom to tell her daughter that she was picked on when she was in school. The goal is to get Anna thinking of her mother every time she tries to pick on Karen. It is helpful to give parents 2-3 specific things they can do or say to their children to help with whatever the phone call is about.

Calling Home to Praise:

Try to make at least two positive calls per week to parents of difficult students. With this type of call there is no need to tell the student ahead of time. Often a surprise Monday night call to praise hard work, leadership, teamwork, etc... will get good behavior for the rest of the week. This type of call can be short and sweet. Be sure to praise the parent on doing a fine job at home with their son or daughter. Again, this goes a long way in being able to utilize parents later on.

Concluding chapter thought:
It is so important to remember that relationships come first. Students will follow us if we take extra time to get to know them as people. Ask yourself the following question: Why did you go into teaching in the first place? Hopefully your answer has the word "kids" or "children" in it. I went into teaching because I wanted to make a difference in the lives of kids who need a positive role model or influence. Do not let content get in the way of students. My students as people come first. My students as learners come second.

CHAPTER TWO

Fair vs. Equal
What it is and how to implement it:

"It's not fair Mr. Mendler, it's just not fair. We both did the same thing but you didn't do nothing to him. How come you're picking on me?" Does this sound familiar? Understanding how to be "fair" without worrying about treating all students exactly the same way was one of the most important things I learned early in my career (Curwin & Mendler, 1988; Mendler, 2005; Mendler et.al 2008). I always knew to differentiate homework, consequences, tests, quizzes, and assignments based on individual student needs. However, I did not know what to do when one student complained about what I did for someone else. This chapter will help you understand what being fair means, how to be fair on a daily basis, and what to do if and when a student complains that you are not being fair.

The Key: The key to this concept is that the teacher makes a commitment to not talking about what he/she is doing for one student to any other student. Just as

---

a doctor does not discuss one patient's medication with another patient, teachers should not discuss one child's consequence, homework, grade, bathroom break, classroom seat, water fountain break (you get the point), with any others in the class. It is also important not to discuss one student with someone else's parent. If a doctor talks to one parent about another child's medication they can lose their license to practice medicine. Think of yourself as the doctor. No matter how hard a student or parent tries to get me to talk about another student I will not.

What the Teacher Needs to do for Students:
Tell them this, "I will always do my absolute best to be *fair* to each and every one of you in this room this year, which means I *will not* worry about treating you all exactly the same way. That means some of you might get different assignments, consequences, tests, quizzes etc... If and when this happens you may not complain I am not being fair. You might say I am not being equal. But I am not promising to be equal in here. I am promising to be fair." I suggest that every teacher write the word *fair* and the word *equal* in a prominent location in your room. Then laminate each on a large sheet of paper.

Fair means that every individual in this class will always get what he or she needs to be successful.

Equal means everyone gets exactly the same thing.

How to implement this on a daily basis:
Students (and most teachers) have learned that *fair* and *equal* mean the same thing. Here is an example of a situation where the teacher assigns different homework based on the needs of each student.

The TAMING of the CREW

Student: I have to do 10 problems and she only has to do 5? That's not fair!

Teacher: I know how many she has. Why can't you do 10?

Student: Because she got...

Teacher (cutting off): I know the assignment she is doing. Are you saying you can't do 10?

Student: But she only has to do 5.

Teacher: I know how many she is doing. I am the one who assigned it. What is wrong with your ten?

Don't bite. Just repeat the phrase, "I know. I am the one who assigned it. What is the problem with your assignment?" Almost always they will tell you about the other student again. If the student continues to complain about his peer simply say, "When you are ready to talk about your assignment (consequence, test, quiz, bathroom break, etc...) I will be glad to listen." And then walk away! Be very clear that you are not willing to talk to one student about another but that you will always talk to the student about the problem they are having.

What if there is bullying? Can a student talk to the teacher about another student if they feel picked on?

Teach students to define the problem as their own. For example, a student getting picked on should say, "Mr. Mendler, I'm scared. I feel like if I walk out of this room right now I am going to get beat up. Can you please help?" This student talks completely about himself. Of course any good teacher follows up with, "Ok. Who is it with and what is it about?" When danger or safety is involved, students need to know that the adults will protect them. It is absolutely okay under these circumstances for kids to come to you.

How the Administrator can Help:

Administrators can be most helpful by supporting teachers that are giving different tests, quizzes, homework assignments and consequences. Try to stay away from policies that require all students to be treated the same way. Instead, use words like "usually," "often", and "most of the time" when creating policies. Encourage teachers to not have a one-size fits all mentality.

Some teachers might not like me for saying this, but I believe administrators should practice the fair/equal concept as well. Tell teachers you will work hard to be *fair* to each and every one of them, which means you will not worry about treating them exactly the same way. Explain it like this: "Some of you might have 30 students and others might have 27. Some might have to teach 6 periods and others only 5. Please do not complain to me that it is not fair. You can complain that it is not equal, but I am not promising to be equal I am promising to be fair." Now the administrator can look at every individual situation before making a decision.

I remember a former principal saying this to us at a faculty meeting: "This is my world. I run it. You all are the president of a country inside my world. This is your classroom, your community. But it is my world. And sometimes your country might be asked to do something for the good of the world that you don't understand, because you are only focused on your country. If you ever really want to know why your country is asked to do something that not all other countries are, I will do my best to explain but I am telling you now the explanation might not make sense to you. Just remember I will not necessarily treat all countries the same."

Fair/Equal and Consistency:
After learning this concept many teachers ask about consistency. They say, "Don't I need to give the same consequence or assignment in order to be consistent?" No! I am as consistent as it gets. I will **never** talk to one student about what I am doing for another student. I will **always** do what I think is best for each individual. I will consistently be fair, which means I consistently will not worry about treating everyone exactly the same way. I will consistently talk to parents about their own child. I will consistently not talk to any parent about someone else's child. Is it possible to be any more consistent than that? Remember, the word consistency means I need to do the same thing. It does not tell me what that thing is.

Remember, Equal often is Fair!
The reason this concept works so well is because most of the time teachers will be equal. You will often give the same assignment, test, quiz, etc... to the entire class. I never said not to be equal. I am just asking you to be fair! The reason we move kids in school based on age is because most are at approximately the same level. Most 8 year-olds read at a 3rd grade level. Most 16 year olds are at a 10th or 11th grade level. But a different tool is needed for the 3rd grader reading at a 6th grade level and the 6th grader reading at a 3rd grade level. Each student gets what he/she needs and we

do not worry about what anyone else says about it.

Eighteen Different Ways to Say the Same Thing:
Practice until they become part of the natural way you respond to students and parents. I used to stand in my shower and practice. I know. It sounds crazy. But it worked!

1. Guys let me explain to you... I will always do my best to be fair in here which means I will not worry about treating you exactly the same way. Isn't that great?
2. This means that you might get one consequence and you might get something different for the exact same behavior! Do not complain to me that it is not fair.
3. You can complain that it's not equal, but I am not promising to be equal in here, I am promising to be fair.
4. What is the problem with what I did for you?
5. I know what I did for him, and you are not him. What is the problem with what I did for you?
6. When you are ready to talk about you I'll listen.
7. Yes it is fair, it's just not equal, please learn the difference!
8. I will be available from ____ to ____. If you come up with something that is going to work better, I will be glad to hear it. But until that time I have to do what I think is best. And I think ____ is best.
9. Even you are telling me it's not going to work. But I hope you come up with something that will!
10. You don't want to do the homework? Ok.

Then you better come up with another way to show me you understand the material.

11. I see where her books are but you need to worry about your books. Thanks for having your books where they are supposed to be.

12. I know she didn't raise her hand, but you need to worry about your hand. Thanks for raising it.

13. I know the grade she got. I am the one who gave it to her. What is the problem with your grade?

14. I know the homework he is doing. What is the problem with your homework?

15. I am not interested in talking to you about her grade but I will talk to you about yours. What do you want to know?

16. I am not interested in talking to you about his assignment but I will talk to you about yours. What do you want to know?

17. I know his head is down and you don't look tired! Why do you need to put your head down?

18. Guys, in my opinion, homework and consequences are nothing more than vehicles to a destination. The destination is not negotiable. How we get there does not matter to me. In fact, I'd rather have you decide!

Seventeen Phrases that Make this Concept Work for Parents:

1. Parents, I need to let you know right now I will always do my best to be fair to each and every one of your children, which means I will not worry about treating them exactly the same way.

2. This means your child might get one consequence and yours might get another for the exact same behavior.
3. If your child ever breaks a rule and you think there is a better consequence that will get your child to not break the rule again, please let me know.
4. You can complain that it is not equal, but I'm not promising to be equal. I am promising to be fair.
5. Just like I would never discuss your son or daughter with another parent, I will not be discussing other children with you. I'm sure you understand that.
6. What is the problem with what I did for your son/daughter?
7. I know what I did for his friend. What is the problem with what I did for your child?
8. When you are ready to talk about your son/daughter I'd be glad to listen.
9. Yes it is fair, it's just not equal!
10. So are you telling me all I have to do is _____ _____ and starting tomorrow your son/daughter will behave?
11. Ok. That's what I'll do. And I trust tomorrow your son/daughter will behave in this class.
12. I'll be available from _____ to _____. If you come up with something that's going to work better, I'd be glad to hear it. But until that time I have to do what I think is best. And I think _____ is best.
13. Well Mrs. _____, even you're telling me it's not going to work. But I hope you come up with something that will!

14. You don't think he should have to do the homework? Can you come up with a different way to show me he understands the material?
15. I know the grade her friend got. What's the problem with your son/daughter's grade?
16. I know the homework his friend is doing. What's the problem with your son's homework?
17. Homework and consequences are nothing more than vehicles to a destination. The destination is not negotiable. How we get there does not matter to me. In fact, I'd rather have you decide!

Teacher Exercise:
• For one week count how many times each day one student complains about what you are doing for someone else. For example, a student says, *"He got 5 problems and I have to do 10? That's not fair."* Or, *"She didn't raise her hand!"* Or, *"When I did that I got a detention, now you are only calling his mom? No way is that fair?"* Most teachers find that students initially say these types of statements between 5 and 30 times per day. Record each in a journal. This exercise will show you how important learning the above phrases are.

• Repeat one or more of the sentences above so you can find the one(s) that feel most natural to you: "I know about her assignment (test, quiz, etc...), I am the one who gave it to her and I am not talking to you about it. But if you have a problem with your assignment (consequence, etc...), please see me later and tell me what you think will work better."

The student will almost always be unable to talk about himself. If she tells you about another student again, the next line will have to be practiced over and over: *"When you are ready to talk about you I will listen!"* This phrase is delivered as a *hit and run.* Practice walking away until it becomes comfortable and a natural way to respond. Students will eventually learn to talk about themselves.

When the Student Learns to Talk About Him or Herself:

This will eventually happen. When a student says, *"I don't think that I should have to do 10 problems tonight for homework,"* do not get into a power struggle by saying *"Yes you will do 10 because I said so."* Instead, practice over and over saying the following: *"Ok. How many problems do you think you need to do to show me you understand the material?"* If the student says none, tell him that is not an option since if he did none you would have no way of knowing whether or not he knows the material. You might negotiate here (i.e. but I can live with five). If the complaint is about a different consequence: *"Ok. What consequence do you think will work best for you?"* Keep your eye on the goal. Remember, we do not have to treat everyone exactly the same way.

Time to Practice:

Here are some scenarios to practice using the above phrases. If you have access to other teachers, practice the scenarios with each person taking on one of the roles. If you do not have access, simply practice on your own.

• Billy and Tommy are both second graders and good friends. Billy is excellent at multiplication but Tommy struggles in this area. The teacher gives Billy 5 homework problems and Tommy 10. Tommy is not happy about it and complains to the teacher that it is not fair. You are the teacher. How do you respond?

• Marissa and Carrie are both in 10th grade and good friends. Yesterday in class they both called the teacher an a**hole. This behavior warrants a consequence, but you want to do what you think will work best for each student. Marissa's mom is not very involved in her education but you know Marissa hates staying after school. Carrie's mom is very involved in her education and you know a phone call home is all it will take for her to behave. So you give Marissa a detention and Carrie a phone call home. Marissa is mad because she knows a phone call home would be like not having a consequence. She complains that it is not fair. How do you respond?

• Amy complains that Stephanie has her head down. How do you respond to Amy?

• Bob complains that Andy gets to make up questions he got wrong on a quiz. How do you respond to Bob?

Fair vs. Equal Practice Parent Scenarios:

• Mr. Thomas is not happy that you gave his son 10 problems and his best friend only got 5. Mr. Thomas calls you and says, *"That's not fair, you gave my son 10 problems and his best friend got 5? Why is my child being punished?"* How do you handle Mr. Thomas?

- Ms. Gonzalez is not happy that her daughter got a detention and her best friend got a phone call home for the same behavior. Ms. Gonzalez calls and says, *"That's not fair, you gave my daughter a detention and you called Carrie's mom? You are not being fair to my daughter."* How do you handle Marissa's mom?

- Amy's mom calls because she can't believe you allowed Stephanie to put her head down in class. She wants to know why that is allowed. How do you handle Amy's mom?

Learning, practicing, and implementing this concept is well worth the work it takes. Although it would be nice if simple one size fits all formulas worked, the reality of teaching is that we have academically and emotionally diverse students who are not all capable of succeeding at the same thing in the same way on the same day. They each need us to be fair without necessarily treating everybody the same.

Concluding Chapter Thought:
The concept of being fair without worrying about treating everyone exactly the same way is the most important concept I adopted in my career. It has allowed me to truly differentiate homework, consequences, tests, quizzes, bathroom breaks, etc... without hearing others complain. It takes a lot of practice to become comfortable with the phrases so do not get discouraged when first learning them. Mastering this concept also allows us to know exactly what to say when parents complain about what we are doing for someone else's child.

CHAPTER THREE

Getting Students to do and Complete Homework

This is not easy and there is no absolute formula to the completion of homework. There are often factors that we have no control over. Parents working late, sports practice, religious school and household chores are just a few things that can and do get in the way. However, I believe there are many specific strategies teachers can use to maximize student potential to do and complete homework. The main point about homework is that kids should see the connection between doing it and how it will benefit them. This may not always be obvious and sometimes they will need to simply trust your judgment. You must therefore have the discretion to give assignments based on what you think will benefit each of your students which is why framing the distinction between being fair and being equal is so important (see chapter 2). Against that backdrop, I offer the following strategies, often in the way I say them to my class.

Prevent Homework Complaining:
This assignment is so stupid!
No way should we have to do this!
I don't understand when I am ever going to use this in my life!

Sound familiar? If so, a simple dialogue between the teacher and class can go a long way in preventing these types of statements.

Try Saying this when Greeting your Class:
Mr. M: Hey class. It's great to meet you. My name is Mr. Mendler and I have to tell you something really important. There is one thing in this world that I hate more than anything else. Pay attention. I hate more than anything when people waste my time. I don't feel like I have enough time as it is. I teach you, I get to teach seminars to teachers, I write books, I teach a graduate school class, and I try to have a few minutes with friends and family. So I hate when people waste my time.
Class: Mr. Mendler, why do we care?
Mr. M: Great question. Here's why you care. Because I hate so much when people waste my time, I promise you right now I will do my best not to waste your time this year. You see, some teachers might mean well, but they end up wasting your time. They give homework every single night of the week even if they have nothing to give! They find something! Not me. I won't do that to you.
Class: So we will never have homework in here?
Mr. M: I didn't say that. Listen closely. On average in this class this year you will have homework 3-4 nights per week. Understand this. When I give homework it is important and needs to get done. You might not like the homework I give and you might not understand why I'm giving it. Let me say that again. You might not, in fact you probably will not always like the homework I am giving and you might not understand why I am giving it. Whenever possible, I will do my best to explain how you will benefit from doing the homework, but

trust me when I tell you this: It is never given to waste your time. Sometimes you might be asked to do things and you might not understand why. But it is my job to prepare you for the future. So remember, I will do my best never to waste your time. I will not give homework just so you are not playing video games or hanging with friends.....By the way, since I promise to try hard not to waste your time, I trust you will try hard not to waste mine. Goofing off in class, not paying attention, yelling out, and being inappropriate... are all things that waste my time. So please do not do it. Otherwise I can start wasting yours. I would just prefer not to.

If three days later students do not have their homework done, instead of getting annoyed and asking where it is, I can simply say, "you know what guys, I thought we talked about wasting time. I planned a lesson last night based on the belief that your homework would be done. I feel like I wasted my time. Do I need to start wasting yours?" Now the discussion becomes about wasting time instead of the completion of work.

This strategy accomplishes two goals. First, we made very clear that there is a purpose behind everything we ask them to do. We are not going to waste their time. Second, students can plan ahead because we have told them, for the most part, which nights assignments will be given.

Try to Give Students a Say:

I have already told the class they will be getting an average of 3-4 nights per week of homework. This is not negotiable. However, asking which nights they might prefer is not a bad idea. We take a secret ballot vote and students write in order from 1-4 the week nights they prefer. Those are the nights I try to give homework. If my class picks Wednesday and the work is not done on Thursday I can say, "aren't you guys the ones who picked Wednesdays? I am very disappointed that you are not able to follow through with what you said you were going to do." There is no argument about incomplete homework.

The Retail Mindset:

Have you ever come home from the store and told your significant other you got a great deal? I hate to burst your bubble, but just because the price tag says 69.99, has a line through it, and says 39.99 does not mean you got a great deal! Just because a shirt is on the "clearance" rack does not make it an amazing buy. But most of us love discounts and sales. We can't help it. So why not put homework and tests on sale every once in a while? In the following example I want my students to do 10 problems but look at what I say:

Mr. M. (as class is about to end): Ok guys. Great job today. Tonight I need you to do numbers 1-20. I'll see your homework tomorrow.

Students: Aw man. Twenty problems? Come on. That's so much!!!!

Mr. M.: Ok. Well how many do you think you should have to do?

Students: Zero.

Mr. M.: Zero is not an option and you know that. But I want 20 and you want zero. What is in between?

Students: Ten.

Mr. M.: Fine. And in fact, why don't you just do

the 10 easiest on the page. Or better yet, do whichever ten are going to best show me you understand the material. But don't forget how nice I am. I will see your homework tomorrow.

If they do not argue the 20, I get more than I really want anyway. If they argue I still get what I want, but the class believes they are getting a deal. Negotiating is a skill rarely taught or practiced in school. I like when students do it. It makes them feel empowered and it costs us nothing, especially when we approach it with the retail mindset. This can be done on tests as well. If you want them to complete a 25 question multiple choice quiz put 35 questions on the test. Then if they complain, pretend you are not happy and "reluctantly" give in to fewer but plenty!

I tell you, you tell me, it's written down, you can go...

Have you ever given a homework assignment, been very clear with your class about what they have to do, and then had a student come the next day without it done? Her reason: "You never told us what the assignment was!" This makes me so frustrated. Other times a parent will call and say "She says you never told her what she was supposed to do!!" So to prevent this, simply implement the three-step technique I learned from Janet Sikes, a fifth grade teacher in Buffalo, NY: Three things must happen every time I give homework before students are allowed to leave my room.

1. First, I tell them the assignment.
2. Second, each repeats it back to me.
3. Third, I see it is written down.

Now we can say this to our class: "Some of you are going to come in unprepared and try to tell me I never told you what the assignment was. In this room, that will not be possible because three things have to happen before you are allowed to leave (tell your students the three things). I am sure you will all agree that if you get home and have forgotten what I told you, forgotten what you told me, and lost the paper it was written down on, you are an irresponsible student. Do you agree?"

I recommend repeating exactly what was said to students with their parents. "Mr. and Mrs. Moms and Dads... three things are required to happen every time I give your child an assignment (see above)." When you set things up this way, instead of calling and complaining that "you never told their child the homework," the phone call is much different. This really happened just a few weeks ago.

"Mr. Mendler, it is Mrs. Carey. I am not happy with Michael. Apparently he forgot what you told him the assignment was. He forgot what he told you, and yes he lost the notebook again. And I promise Mr. Mendler, we are working on it. Can you please tell me the assignment again so I can help him?"

Having a system in place like this leads to a very different tone from most parents. Of course I am now willing to tell Mrs. Carey the assignment again. And she is not pleased with her son, which is not necessarily a bad thing.

Focus on outcomes and quality instead of quantity!

Many teachers spend too much time caring about what the homework is. It is of far greater importance to focus on the outcome of the homework. When assigning, state clearly what skill(s) you want them to learn. What is the purpose of the assignment? If a student already knows how to multiply does he really need to do 25 problems to show you? Some teachers believe that doing the 25 will give the student much needed practice. I am not against this, but be sure the student really does need the practice. After all, how many times do you need to practice 9 x 9 before it starts getting annoying?

Lists for Responsibility:
Jema Bethlendy, a fifth grade teacher in Brighton, NY requires her students to make a written list of all after school and homework responsibilities when they get home along with how much time each is likely to take. She assists by telling her students how much time on average each school assignment should take. The teacher grades the list every morning which ensures students will create one. The goal is for students to see the importance of the list and begin doing it on their own without being graded. Students are expected to number each task from most important to least. As the student finishes a task it is crossed out. Below is an example of a Thursday afternoon list from Payton, a fifth grader in this class.
1. Math Worksheet (10 min)
2. Writing (10 min)
3. Reading (15 min)
4. Grandmothers birthday dinner (have to go)
5. Cheerleading practice (1 hr)
6. Instrument practice
7. Practice for spelling quiz (10 min)

With the tasks in front of her, Payton can now begin completing them. Some (grandmother's dinner and practice spelling) can be done at the same time. The parentheses are for the amount of time each should take. Naturally, this varies somewhat based upon each student's talents and needs. This student is already really good at spelling so she probably does not need the full 10 minutes. This night the instrument did not get practiced. With this structure, students can plan extra time on Friday or during the weekend for certain tasks not completed during the week.

Homework can be a battleground and the source of major power struggles with kids. Be sure to try including students in decisions regarding homework. When we focus on outcomes, what we want them to learn, instead of how much they do, this becomes a lot easier.

Concluding Chapter Thought:

Remember that homework should be viewed primarily as a vehicle to a destination. The destination or outcome of the homework (understanding multiplication, writing sentences, improved reading) should not be negotiable. How each student gets there (the vehicle or amount of homework) might be different for each student (differentiated instruction). I became a better teacher the day I stopped caring so much about the amount of homework being done and began caring much more about the learning each student derived from the homework.

CHAPTER FOUR

Creative Teaching Strategies and Motivational Tips

Fresh ideas keep the job exciting and students on their toes. This is what makes teaching fun. If we are constantly doing the same boring, monotonous things every day, many students lose interest. This chapter is dedicated entirely to these ideas. They are designed to energize your lessons and motivate your students. Some of them I invented. Many others I stole from outstanding educators all over the country who shared them during seminars or on-site consultation. I apologize for not always remembering the source of a wonderful idea.

EBAY for Economics?

A colleague and I set up an EBAY account under our names. For homework, our students (with parental permission) looked for items that were taking up space at their house or in their yards. They brought them in and listed each on EBAY. From start to finish students took pictures, downloaded them to the computer, wrote a description, decided how long the auction should last, packaged and mailed the item. Students kept any money they generated from the sale of their items.

Student interest in economics skyrocketed. Other teachers began bringing items to our room. Our class listed the other teachers' items from start to finish and took a small percentage of the profit for themselves. We believed there was no better way to teach economics. To this day I have former students thanking me for teaching a skill they have been able to continue to use. One student from that class is now an EBAY Power Seller and makes over 40 thousand dollars per year!

Many schools have a bookstore operated by students that sell shirts, snacks, etc... This too is a great way to use real life business to teach basic economics.

Blue Light Special:

This comes from Jenny Estl in Omaha, NE. Borrowing from a well-known K-mart practice, she decided to buy a blue light for her classroom. When she turns it on her students are allowed to do make up work at no penalty. This includes any tests, quizzes, or papers, etc... The goal is to get students caught up when they are drastically behind. Her "good students" that do not have any make-up work get extra credit for helping their classmates.

Number Coded Tasks:

This comes from Sonya in Cleveland OH. In her 3rd grade room students often need to use the bathroom or get a drink. So she number codes those two actions. For example, if a student needs to use the bathroom they raise their right hand with the pointer finger in the air. If they need to get a drink it is the left hand pointer finger. This helps students learn the difference between right and left. It also allows the teacher to understand what her students want without asking. She can then respond with a quick, "hurry up", or "wait three minutes until I'm finished".

She uses this technique with other tasks as well. If kids do not understand a concept and need it reviewed again, they raise their right hand in a fist. If they have a specific question that needs to be asked about what she is teaching it is the left hand in a fist. Each coded task is clearly labeled and posted in the room. Sonya says it is amazing how quickly the kids learn right from left, and also how much more she is able to accomplish by knowing ahead of time what her students want when hands go up.

Real sign language can be substituted if the teacher knows it.

Opposite Day:

Opposite day is created by Melissa Haufner in Columbus, Ohio. She works with some very difficult and hostile students that often come to class with bad attitudes. Every once in a while, when she notices the students are especially upset, she announces it is "opposite day". This means anything anyone says in the room means the opposite. For example, if a student is mad and says, "this class sucks" it really means, "this class is great," and Melissa responds as if the latter were said. She says something like this to the student, "I'm glad you are enjoying class so much. If you want me to think you are miserable, be sure to say you are in a great mood!" If nothing else this strategy gives the teacher a way to feel better when kids are blatantly rude and disrespectful. Opposite day works best when it is spontaneously used by the teacher.

Some of the next several strategies are adapted from Mendler, Curwin and Mendler (2008) and are especially helpful when working with ADHD students.

The Power of Velcro and Tape:

Place a piece of Velcro or tape underneath the chair of your students who have ADHD. Tell the student to rub the velcro when they start getting antsy. The stimulation they feel from touching often focuses kids with ADHD.

Music Stands and ADHD:

This is a great idea! Go to the music room and borrow 4 or 5 music stands. Spread them around the back of your room and let students know they can work at their desk or at the music stand. The stands can be raised or lowered to meet any height. They have a hard writing surface and most even have a ledge that can hold pens, paper, notebooks, etc...

Pen Tapper and Carpet:

Have you noticed there are actually two different types of pen tappers? The first type taps to intentionally drive us crazy. This strategy does not work for them. But the second type (approximately 50% of all tappers), are tapping for an entirely different reason. They are often engrossed in deep thought and not aware of what they are doing. How do you know the difference between the two different types of pen tappers? When you ask them to stop one does and is genuinely sorry. Then 10 seconds later is tapping again. A few years ago I walked into my classroom and my paraprofessional had a long scrap of carpeting. I looked at her and asked what she was doing with

the carpet. She told me that she was sick of hearing me tell kids to "stop tapping their pens." She then told me she was going to place a small piece of carpet held down with duct tape to each desk. She said, "Bri, is it the pen tapping that drives you crazy, or the noise from the pen tapping that drives you crazy?" It was the noise. She then said, "If I kill the noise will you stop whining?" As our students walked in she said, "guys, do me a favor. I am sick of hearing Mr. Mendler complain. Please tap on the carpet." Most did, and for the most part the problem was solved.

Exercise Bouncy Balls:

This one takes some guts and courage. Adrienne Amos, a teacher in Des Moines Iowa, decided to replace all the chairs in her room with exercise bouncy balls. Her students had a constant need for movement and she was sick of them leaning back in their chairs. She said one boy actually leaned back too far and his chair tipped over leaving him with a minor lump on the back of his head. "They were always moving so I decided I'd give them a way to move right at their desks." I asked her if the kids bounced around the room. She said that most of the bouncing was done right in place behind the desk. She said the amount of disruption decreased significantly with the new bouncy ball chairs. This teacher also pointed out that not only did they bounce in place, but the bouncing in place was noiseless which eased her tension on a daily basis.

Physical Therapy Half Moon:

Some of us might not be able to get away with exercise bouncy balls. So finding a way for some kids to bounce in place can work well. Some physical therapy stores sell "half moon" exercise balls. Picture the full ball sliced in half with one side completely flat. These can

be placed on top of a student desk so he can bounce right in place.

Killing Sliding-Desk Noise:

Cutting slits in tennis or racquet balls and sliding them over the metal ends will eliminate chair noise when students slide the desks back and forth. Just be sure to secure the balls on the chairs or some students will pull them off. Home Depot and Loews sell felt tips that can be placed over the metal part of the desk as well... for easy sliding.

Swimming Noodles:

Do you have any students that swing their feet back and forth, occasionally kicking the chair or student in front of them? The long styrofoam noodles that kids use to float around in swimming pools can help. I recently met a teacher that cuts the noodle in half and places it at the feet of the leg swinger. Watch the student use her feet to roll the noodle back and forth without even knowing it. This is great because the noodles are cheap, cannot hurt anyone, and do not make any noise. Three qualities all teachers love. Now instead of kicking the student or chair in front, she can roll the noodle back and forth.

Kids Design the Classroom:

I like my desks in a horseshoe shape so students can hear and see each other. That being said, this next strategy is a fun way for students to share some ownership of their classroom design. A teacher I met in New Hampshire allows her students to choose from four different classroom design options. The class votes on how they want the room arranged. It stays that way for 2 weeks. After two weeks the class votes again. Remember, they are always voting on different designs created by the teacher.

Songs that teach?

Almost all of us are good at remembering lyrics to catchy songs, even if that song is not our favorite. Some teachers have been very successful at teaching content by writing a song for the concept they are teaching.

This first song comes from a teacher in Amsterdam, N.Y. Her students were forgetting how to add and subtract numbers with different signs, and which sign went in front of the answer (i.e.-8 + 3). So she created a song to the tune *Row Row Row Your Boat*. It goes like this:

Same sign add and keep,
Different sign subtract...
Take the sign of the highest number
Then you'll be exact!

The second song is from Quando Dennis, a teacher at Captial City Alternative School in Jackson, MS. Ms. Dennis is a Science teacher and created a song called "In a Cell" to the tune of "Jingle Bells."
It goes like this:

In a cell, in a cell, there is so much stuff
Cytoplasm, cell membrane, and a
nucleuuuuuuus!
In a cell, in a cell, the nucleus is in control...
And outside a cell membrane, the cytoplasm
holds!

Place content or review material into a song with a catchy tune and watch test scores soar!

Quotes or inspirational sayings on the wall:

If you attended one of my seminars you know what I am about to say. I believe in the power of positive people and I try to surround myself with such. Maybe this has become especially important because I primarily teach unmotivated, disrespectful, and disruptive kids. In large part, I see my job as trying to inspire these students to believe in themselves. I try to let them know in lots of ways that they have what it takes to be successful in school and in life! So how do I manage this? I engulf my room and students in positive sayings, inspirational quotes, and "can-do" messages. This idea came in my second year of teaching. I was working in a middle-class district, teaching a smattering of inclusion and self-contained. My building had positive quotes wrapped like a banner around the top of the school. Each quote and its author was stenciled into the wall in a very creative, artsy way. At the beginning of the semester I took my class on a field trip around the school. Their job was to wander the halls and write down their top ten quotes, and the author of each. When we came back each wrote their favorites on the board. We then decided on the class' favorite ten. The top ten were stenciled (with permission of course) on to the walls of our room.

The class then did a writing project where each explained why she liked the quote, what it meant personally, and how it could be applied to her life. This assignment almost always generated a 100% completion rate. It also had students interested in learning things about people they never would have considered.

Some of my Favorites and who said them:
"I have taken more than 9000 shots in my career. I have lost almost 300 games. On 26 occasions I have been trusted to take the game winning shot... and missed. And I have failed over and over and over again in my life, and that is why... I succeed."
-Michael Jordan

"No matter how good you get you can always get better and that's the exciting part!"
-**Tiger Woods**

"Our greatest glory is not in never falling but in rising every time we fall."
-**Confucius**

"To climb steep hills requires a slow pace at first."
-**Shakespeare**

Reminders for Students:

Some students need reminders for what, how, and why they are doing something.
Here are a few examples of some reminder phrases and strategies.

"Deposit All Trash Talk Here"

My dad wrote about this in one of his earlier books. This quote is written on a nerf basketball hoop a high school physics teacher has in his room. Under the hoop is a trash can. Any time a student uses inappropriate language, instead of stopping his lesson; he crumples up a sheet of paper and throws it at the can as a reminder to leave all trash talk at the door.

"Laminated Stop Sign at the Door"

This comes from a teacher in Toledo, OH. She has a big laminated stop sign on her door. Under the sign is a list of all materials students needed to bring with them to class.

**Reminders for the Teacher:
"ABT and NBP"**
"Always Be Teaching and Never Be Punishing." A teacher I used to work with walked around the building saying this all day. "ABT, ABT, ABT. No matter what a student does or says, *always be teaching.* If they don't know how to walk in the hall, show them how. If they don't know how to make eye contact, show them how. If they don't know how to say please and thank you, well somebody better show them! ABT and NBP Bri. Always be teaching, never be punishing."

"Promise me you will always do what is best for kids"
This came from my mom. She was the director of special education during my first year as a special education teacher which made her my boss. She made every teacher promise we would make every decision every day based on what we thought was in the best interest of a child. After we promised her we would do what was best for kids, she promised us two things. If you always do what you think is best for kids there will always be a place for you in education and you will be very successful. And remember this, she advised: If you always do what you think is best for kids you will make some people angry along the way.

"Stay personally connected to students without taking personally what they do and say"
My dad (Mendler, A. 2007) considers this to be a key attitude in being successful with difficult students. Remember to always stay personally connected to every student you teach, without taking personally what they do or say. This is not easy to do. But when mastered,

it changes the way we teach. For example, let's say Jon tells me, "Mr. Mendler you are the worst teacher ever and I hate you!" If I can stay personally connected to the student without taking personally what he says, I am much more able to respond like this: "You know what Jon, I hear you are angry right now and are needing to express your displeasure. I'm not sure what it is that has you furious with me, but I'd be happy to hear about it after class. Thanks for sharing your concern." Notice there is no power struggle, the situation is diffused, and we can move forward with the lesson. We also acknowledged his feelings and gave him a time to talk to us later. Almost always when a student calls us a name or says something inappropriate, it is not about us. There is almost always something else going on in that child's life that is the catalyst for his anger.

"Sports, Music, Video Games, Money"

Every student likes at least one of these four. Figuring out how to incorporate these interests into a lesson can inspire and motivate. I am reminded of a 7th grade math colleague with whom I co-taught. I was the inclusion special education teacher and Jennifer the general education teacher. She was the best I have ever seen at incorporating student interests into lessons.

One Monday the students are chatting at the beginning of class about the extremely popular television show American Idol. Two of them are talking about how when they grow up they want to be just like Paula and Randy (two of the judges on the show). Jennifer overhears the conversation, looks directly at the class and says, "you do not want to be like them.

No way. You want to be like Simon (the third judge). Do you guys know Simon is the Executive Producer of the show? Do you know every person that signs up to even try out for that show has to sign a two year record contract with his label? Do you know that in 6 years of that show he has brought in more money than the Rolling Stones did in their entire career? Do you know Simon actually can get rid of Randy or Paula any time he wants? Randy and Paula are okay but you want to be Simon.

Jennifer of course is showing these numbers to the class. She finishes, looks at the class and says, ok... enough talking about American Idol. Now we need to get some math done! Let's go. We will talk more about that show tomorrow."

She was the best I have ever seen at turning student talking into a lesson. I asked Jennifer how she knew so much about that show. She looked at me and said, "I don't. I make half of it up. But I sound good, don't I? And it's not like the students ever check my facts!!!" So true.

"QTIP"

My dad reminded me of this all the time in my first and second year of teaching. Remember QTIP when a student says something rude, nasty or inappropriate. **Q**uit **T**aking **I**t **P**ersonally! This is good advice to pass along to your students as well when somebody says something to them they do not like.

Concluding Chapter Thought:

My paycheck never changes. Whether I am in a good mood or bad, happy or sad, mad or glad, it is always the same. So I figure I might as well have fun when I teach. Using creative strategies helps us continue to enjoy a job that at times can be overwhelming and exhausting. Continue adding to this chapter! The more creative strategies the better our lessons and the more engaged our students. Please email me with creative lessons and ideas that you use with students!

CHAPTER FIVE

Test or Quiz Strategies to Implement Immediately

The goal of this chapter is to enhance learning, spark motivation and make behavior management better during tests and quizzes. I think it is possible to add fun to a time that is often filled with anxiety and tension. Let's explore how.

Wild Card Question:

This comes from Andrea Costa, a 9th grade science teacher in Rochester, NY. On every test or quiz, her students get a wild card question. Sometimes they may have studied a section of material she didn't ask. With the wild card, students can cross out any one question that was asked on the test. In its place they need to write a question they wished would have been asked and answer it correctly. Wild Card can also be used for bonus points if the student answers all questions Andrea asked.

Do you ever allow students to correct their own work, tests, or quizzes?

Yes, but not often. More on that in a moment, but be sure not to have students switch papers and correct each other. Test and quiz scores are confidential

---

information and are not for the teacher to be sharing. However, occasionally having students correct their own work shows we trust them. Once in awhile I'll even allow them to change any one answer they had wrong.

50/50 and Ask the Teacher:

On the game show "Who wants to be a millionaire?," contestants get a limited number of lifelines that allow them to stay in the game. A teacher I recently observed in Georgia allows each student two lifelines on a test or quiz. The first is a 50/50. On one of the multiple-choice questions, students get to use this lifeline. Each student can individually approach the teacher who crosses out two of the wrong answers, leaving two choices to guess from. The teacher that recommends this strategy will allow the student to tell her if they know one of the choices is incorrect. She then crosses out a different answer, leaving the student with a very good chance of correctly answering the question.

"Ask the Teacher" is another lifeline that students are given. At the end of a test, each student can request an answer from the teacher to a question they did not know. A slight variation of this is "Ask a Peer." A student can ask a peer instead of the teacher. I prefer ask the teacher though. It is a bit easier to pull off in a real classroom.

Students Help Write Test Questions:

The day before the test or quiz have each student write two questions they would ask if they were the teacher. That night put all the questions together into a test or quiz. The next day offer them a choice. They can either take the test or quiz the teacher wrote, or the test or quiz their peers wrote. Sometimes you might give them five minutes to look over both versions before they choose. I'm sure you can think of a ton of variations to this strategy as well. One variation created by Jon Smith, a 7th grade teacher follows:

Two Tests, Pick One:

Mr. Smith gives his 7th graders five minutes to look over two different tests. One of the tests is created by him and the other by the students during review time. Three days before the test students are placed in groups. Each group is given a different topic within the bigger unit. Each group then writes four to six test questions pertaining to their topic. The student questions are turned into a test. Mr. Smith also makes a test. The day of the exam each student gets both tests. They get five minutes to look them over and then decide which they prefer to take. Mr. Smith tells me sometimes the student test is actually harder than his!

Index Card?

My friend and teacher Damian Maia in Arkansas came up with this. Give each student a 4x6 note card and allow them to cram as many notes as possible on it before a test or quiz. When filling up the card, students are studying the material while simultaneously deciphering the most important information. Each student is allowed to use the card on the test. Damian says test scores have gone way up because students remember the information they reviewed but left off the card, having spent a lot of time thinking about putting it on.

Get them an easy grade and learn from students?

Once in a while, if my class has been working hard all week I'll surprise them on their end of week quiz. The strategy I'm about to share accomplishes two goals. First, it gets the class an easy quiz grade (which some students will really appreciate). Second, it is an opportunity for me to learn from them. Say this:

"Ok class. Take out a sheet of paper for the quiz. I'm really glad you studied hard and that you are all ready. However, today the quiz is only going to be four questions. Questions 1 and 2: I want you to tell me two things that I do as a teacher that you really like. Questions 3 and 4: I want you to tell me two things as a teacher that you think I can improve. That's it. That's your quiz. Have a great weekend and thanks for working so hard this week!"

Read their suggested improvements. Occasionally you will notice a pattern. For example, one thing many of my students say is that I'm intimidating. They say they love my energy and enthusiasm but sometimes I scare them. If you notice a pattern, address it with your class. For example:

"Hey guys. Thanks for taking the quiz on Friday. I noticed a few of you think I can be intimidating. I appreciate your feedback. Do any of you know what the word 'passionate' means.....? It means I care. I care probably as much or more than anyone in your life. And when people care as much as I do sometimes their voice gets loud, their face gets red, and the veins in their neck bulge out. I'm really sorry if I intimidate you. That is not my intention. But just like you're not always perfect, neither am I. I'll keep working on it. Again, thanks for the feedback. By the way, you all got hundreds on the quiz. Great job."

You can Always Make up the Test, Quiz, Homework, Lab, etc...:

I am often asked: "Do you allow your students to make up tests, quizzes, homework, labs, etc...?" My answer: "Yes. Always." The entire goal of school is for students to do work and for me to help make them better at what they did. One year I was accepting summer reading assignments (due the first day of school) in May! How can I do that? By not predetermining the outcome of late work, tests, quizzes, etc... Allow me to explain. The problem many teachers face is they predetermine an outcome for make-up work. For example, they tell their class, "you can make up your work in here, but you can only earn up to 50% of your original grade." Or, "You can hand in an assignment late but you lose 10 points each day!" If this is you, it's ok. Just go into work tomorrow and change your policy. Why? If a student gets a 30% on the first quiz and can only earn up to 50% of that on the make-up the highest grade possible is a 45%. What is the point of doing the make-up quiz? Either way they fail. Other teachers tell their class they can always make up any work for full credit. This is not good either because some students will not work hard the first time, knowing they can just make it up. So what do you do instead?

Teacher: You can always do make-up work in this class. In fact, I always encourage you to make up all assignments even if you did well. After all, a 90% is outstanding, but it still means you missed 10% of the material.

Student: Well what grade will we get if we do the work?

Teacher: I have no idea.

Student: You have no idea? Why?

Teacher: Because the score you receive on the make-up work will be based on a whole bunch of things. It will be based on how hard you worked the first time and how hard you worked the second time. It will be based on how good your attitude was the first time and how good your attitude was the second time. After the make-up work (test, quiz, writing assignment, lab, etc...) is complete, you and I will sit down together and determine a grade we both think you deserve. Sound good?

Now there is incentive for all students to make up any work they miss. Students who might disrupt to cover academic inadequacy might think twice before disrupting, knowing their make-up test, quiz, or homework assignment is partially based on how hard they worked the first time, and how well they behaved the first time. Instead of having an incentive to disrupt class (so I don't look stupid in front of my peers), I have incentive not to (my behavior right now, will affect my grade in the future).

Concluding Chapter Thought:

It is rare to find a student that actually enjoys taking tests. Implementing some of these strategies will not make students love tests and quizzes, but will hopefully make them a bit more motivated knowing there are a lot of ways they can improve and succeed. Tests and quizzes have and always will be a major part of our education system. They are an important way for students to gain feedback about their learning and for us to get feedback about our teaching. We might at least make them as enjoyable and engaging as possible!

CHAPTER SIX

Values/Rules

I am not going to spend a ton of time writing about values and rules. The latest edition of *Discipline with Dignity* (2008) goes into great detail on this topic. Many classrooms in which I consult struggle to understand the difference between values and rules, so here it is.

A value is broad, general, and explains *why* a certain rule should be followed. A rule is narrow, specific, and explains *what* the person should do. Rules should always be tied directly to values. For example, "All students have the right to feel safe in this classroom." Safety is the value. Based on the value of safety, "All students will keep hands and feet to themselves." Either hands and feet are to themselves or they are not. This is measurable. Remember, students do not have to like a rule and do not have to agree with it either, but a well written rule cannot be argued.

My mom was always really good at understanding the difference between values and rules when we were kids. She told my brother and me that our rooms needed to be cleaned (value). This meant our beds made, laundry folded, carpet vacuumed, and furniture dusted (specific rules that are measurable). I do not recall her saying we had to agree with the rules or that we had to like them. In fact, I distinctly remember her saying she didn't care if we liked them, but that we were not going outside to play until the bedrooms were clean (more on consequences to follow).

The airline industry is remarkable at understanding the difference. Do you know the number one value of every airline? Do not even consider saying "customer service" because it isn't even close. The number one value of all airlines is safety. Based on this value there are rules. Shoes need to come off when going through security. Either they are on or they are off. If you do not want to take them off you don't have to fly. Once on board the flight attendant identifies safety as the main value and then specifies the rules:

1. Seat belts must be fastened.
2. Seatbacks and tray tables in their full, upright and locked position.
3. All electronic devices turned off.

Notice the value is based on attitude and the rule is based on behavior. Schools work best when they follow the same pattern.

Here are a few examples:

- Value - This classroom will be clean before you leave.
- Rule(s) - All papers need to be off the floor.
  - Your chair needs to be on top of your desk.
  - All notebooks, pens, and pencils inside your desk.
- Value - Everyone works hard in this classroom.
- Rule(s) - Each student tells me two specific things you learned today in class.
  - Homework is handed in the day it is due.

- Value - We will tolerate others even when disagreeing.
- Rule – Students will shake hands after an argument.

How do I do it in my classroom?
I determine the values. Students have a say in creating rules.

Mr. M.: Respect is very important in this classroom this year. It is a major value that we all will live by. There are three things you are required to respect in this classroom.
1. Yourself.
2. Each other.
3. This place.

Based on the value of respect, we need to come up with some specific rules we can follow. Who has some ideas?
This is what we came up with:
1. I will never take anything out of anyone else's desk without their permission.
2. I will hang up coats, sweatshirts, or hats before class starts.
3. I will raise my hand before calling out.

It is beneficial to have rules for the teacher as well. Based on the value of respect:
1. I will return your papers within 48 hours of you handing them in.
2. I will not call home without telling you first, unless it is for something positive.
3. I will ask your permission before I post any graded work or assignments for all to see.

Mr. M.: Another major value we will live by in this room this year is responsibility. There are only three things you are required to be responsible for. They are:

1.   Yourself.
2.   This classroom.
3.   This school.

That's it. I will be responsible for everyone and everything else. You worry about yourself, this classroom, and the school. Based on the value of responsibility, we need to come up with some rules we can all live by.

Notice the "I will" statements: By phrasing it this way we give each student individual ownership.

1.   I will bring a notebook and pen every day.
2.   I will make sure my area of the floor is free of all papers and garbage before it is time to go home.
3.   I will tell Mr. Mendler (privately if I want) if I hear there might be a fight.

Based on the Value of Responsibility, here are a Couple of Rules for the Teacher:

1.   I will be on time and begin teaching when the bell rings.
2.   I will help clean up the room at the end of the day.

The Best Way to get Students to Follow Rules:
Student: Mr. Mendler, I think it is so stupid that we can't wear jackets in here. It is totally ridiculous.
Mr. M: I agree. And if I was in charge I would probably let you. But I'm not. So please take your jacket off. If

you want to get a rule changed, Mr. Ackroyd's office (principal) is right down there. I suggest you make an appointment and talk with him about it. But until it is changed, I have to do my job and ask you take it off. Sorry. I really am.

By agreeing the student has nothing left to say. Some administrators ask if it undermines their authority by responding this way. I don't know. Do I have to agree with every rule in society? No. Do I have to follow them or might I get in trouble? Yes. My students know that I don't agree with every rule. I now have the ability to teach a student what to do if they want to get a rule changed. One elementary teacher I know spent time during English writing letters to the principal about their belief that hats should be allowed.

Wouldn't it be nice if police officers did this?
Officer: "Sir, here is your ticket for speeding."
Driver: I can't believe this. That speed limit is way too high. It shouldn't be 40 it should be 65!
Officer: I totally agree and you might be right. But unfortunately, between 5 and 11, I get paid to patrol this area and give people tickets if they are breaking the law. Sorry. If you want to get the speed limit changed I advise calling our state capitol. Again, I am sorry, but I do not make the speed limits, I just enforce them. Have a nice day.

There is nothing left to say. No argument to have. He agrees with me. Agreeing with students when they complain about rules often produces the same results.

Some other Things to Remember About Rules and Values:

- Values are more important. We want students to adopt and live by them. Focus on values.
- Try to get your class to agree on the rules. Values are not negotiable.
- Be sure the rules tell specifically *what* a student, or the teacher, should do.
- Be sure the values tell *why* a student, or teacher, should do it.
- Emphasize or work on a certain rule each week. Once you see significant improvement focus on a new rule.
- Try to write rules in a positive way. Starting with the words "I will" helps.
- Be sure to revisit rules every once in awhile to make sure they still make sense and are valid.
- Do not be afraid to change a rule or even get rid of it completely if it is outdated.

Concluding Chapter Thought:

Although I just finished writing about rules, I am going to change everything on you! Instead of using the word "rule" begin using the word "expectation." The word "expectation" has a very different connotation from the word "rule." An "expectation" trusts a student to do something. "I expect you to walk in the halls. I expect you to keep your hands and feet to yourself." Compare this to, "No running in the halls, or no hitting other people." The latter implies we think the student won't do something. Be sure to remember that an expectation or rule needs to be specific, make sense, and can be measured. The rule or expectation should always tell a student specifically *what* to do. The value should explain *why* they are doing it.

CHAPTER SEVEN

Consequences/Punishments
What happens if they break rules

A consequence is intended to teach better behavior. A punishment is intended to inflict misery. It is very important to understand the difference. A consequence is a natural outcome of a behavior, which means that based on the definition it cannot be predetermined. It can however, be anticipated. It is possible to anticipate that someone will make a mess, what the impact of that will be and what should happen if and when that behavior occurs. But remember, if the behavior didn't happen yet, how can we know the outcome? A punishment is usually decided ahead of time and given in sequential format. Kids need consequences. I am for them and use them often. Consequences involve thought, and most importantly they involve teaching a better, more appropriate way to behave.

I rarely punish. For many of my students it is hard to make their lives more miserable than they already are. In most schools, traditional "consequences" like detention, in-school suspension, and suspension" are misused and end up as punishments. In this chapter I will explain how to use consequences effectively to teach better behavior.

Working Successfully with Difficult Students   69

Why Predetermining Consequences is Almost Never a Good Thing:

Did you hear about the 13 year old girl in Illinois that was given two detentions for hugging her friend good-bye before the weekend? The district's policy did not allow any public displays of affection. The predetermined consequence was a detention. If the detention was skipped the student was then suspended for a day. When asked, the superintendent said that he thought it was *fair* and administrators were just following the policy which stated, "Displays of affection should not occur on the school campus at any time. It is in poor taste, reflects poor judgment, and brings discredit to the school and the persons involved." If this guy was the superintendent in my district I would not be pleased. The policy says? Hey Mr. Superintendent, you are the superintendent. If you have a bad policy, change it!

Do you control your policies or do your policies control you?

When policies control people schools become bad places. If every teacher, administrator, or superintendent makes a decision because a policy says so then why do they need me? Just hire a robot, program it, and put it in my place.

The policy in Illinois was not written with any gray area. A good policy provides guidance and leaves room for discretion. It should have said, "Some displays of affection should not occur at any time. They might be viewed as poor taste, and occasionally will discredit the school and persons involved. If and when this happens, the offending student will at the least be reminded about the behavior and why it is not appropriate. Any further action(s) or consequence(s) will be at the discretion of administration and will be based on what if anything is needed to help the student not break the rule again (remember fair/equal?)." Now the district can use the policy with some discretion. If written this way, common sense would prevail and the girl might actually have been commended for caring enough to hug a friend in need.

An even more intense example is offered to show the danger of being locked into predetermined consequences. I worked at a school with a policy that said, "Any time students fight they will automatically get a five day suspension." On the surface this seemed fine. However, my student, Dan, was a star basketball point guard, and also a gang member. The back-up point guard, Miguel, was in a rival gang. On the court they were friends. Off the court they wouldn't even look at each other. It was bizarre. Anyway, Miguel's friends were trying to get Dan into a fight. They knew that fighting results in a five day suspension and Miguel would become the starter. The basketball coach and I had worked relentlessly teaching Dan, a boy with impulse control problems and a short fuse, how to stay out of a fight. We role-played and discussed specific things he could do and say if enticed. One day he walked out of my room and was pushed in the back. He turned around and said, "Yo man. I'm trying to stay out of trouble. I don't want to fight." He took a step away and got shoved again from behind. Dan turned around and said, "I'm not fighting! I need to stay out of trouble." As Dan turned to walk away again, he was punched in the back of the head and fell into a locker. Dan turned around and knocked the rival gang member out with one punch as I was running to the scene. I looked at Dan and he said, "Mr. Mendler, I tried to walk away. Twice I tried but I got pushed twice and punched in the back of the head. What do you expect me to do?"

Following the policy, my principal suspended Dan for five days. Unfortunately, this taught Dan never to walk away from a fight again. Dan said it to me as he was dejectedly leaving school that day. "Mr. Mendler, I might as well knock him out right away next time. Why take two pushes, a punch, and a bunch of insults when I'm getting suspended either way?" By suspending Dan without considering the circumstances, my principal unraveled all the work we had done with him on walking away. A better fighting policy should say: "Most of the time when people fight there will be a five day suspension. However, every situation will be looked at individually. We will look at who started the fight, who tried to walk away, as well as a bunch of other factors. The final consequence(s) will be determined by the teacher, principal, and any other faculty member involved in the incident. It will always be made by people, not by policies. And remember, the consequence might be different for each individual!"

What Many Predetermined "Consequences" Look Like:

In most schools they look something like this:

1st offense:	Warning
2nd offense:	Phone call home
3rd offense:	Detention
4th offense:	Extended detention
5th offense:	In school suspension
6th offense:	Suspension

If you have consequences predetermined like this I want you to walk up to your most challenging student and say this:

Hi, my name is Mr. Mendler. It is a pleasure to meet you. I just want to let you know right now that the consequence system in this school will be completely ineffective for you this year. In fact, I promise it won't work!

If number one is always a warning why not just stand at the door and hand out thirty free disruption coupons as students come in, because we are giving a free one. Many kids love this because their best disruption can come first. I once observed a student actually say, *"Go ahead. Tell me I shouldn't do it again. You have to warn me. It was my first offense. I'll wait while you warn!"* Number two was a phone call home? For many their parents are the problem! Number three a detention? Some have those lined up from April 1st on. They have so many detentions it is hard to keep them all straight.

I remember in 4th grade I had this teacher named Ms. F. I think she hated us. If you hate kids there are other professions! Anyway, I remember it was a Monday morning and I decided on Sunday night that Monday would be "bring your own chalk to school day." I did something extremely disruptive first thing Monday morning and Ms. F. got up really fast to write my name on the board. But before she got there I said, "Wait, wait, wait, let me do that for you." I walked over to the board, took out my chalk, and wrote the name BRIAN. I took a few steps back toward my seat, looked at her and said, "Let me make the entire week a lot easier for you right now." Next I wrote check marks down the entire board beside my name: about 15 of them. I walked directly up to Ms. F., looked her in the eye, and said, "Is that what they teach you how to do in teacher school? You learn how to write our names and put check marks? Is that what you get your thousands of dollars a year for? Because let me tell you, it isn't going to work!"

Ms. F. kicked me out of class to the principal. I remember him giving me in-school suspension. I laughed. He asked why I was laughing. I told him, "because I am nine and already smarter than you. I love in-school suspension. I hate class. Telling me I'm not allowed to go is not a consequence, it is a reward!"

Let's get this straight. In most schools, the rules tell me I am not allowed to miss class, I should not come late to class, you do not want me to cut class, and the consequence is that I am not allowed to go to class? Do you see the insanity in this? I saw it when I was nine! What was the next consequence? Out of school suspension? "Whatever. I'll worry about that when I get there. I still have four solid disruptions until then!" There is your sequenced system of consequence for many difficult kids.

So does that mean we should not give consequences?

No. That is not what it means. Students need consequences! In fact, I use all of the above consequences often. I am just against you telling me the order I have to use them. Leave your consequence list up and take your numbered order down. Some disruptive behaviors do not warrant a warning. Many know exactly what they are doing, do it intentionally, and I am not warning them for it. If number one is a warning then I have to warn. Calling home is ineffective for many students. Detention works for kids with good home lives who hate staying after school. In-school suspension works for those who enjoy being in class. Do we ever need to suspend students? Yes, primarily when safety is an issue. But please understand that every time we suspend a student we do our community a disservice. Do you think suspended students are home composing a well written paper on how to improve behavior upon return? Of course not. They play video games, hang out at the mall, movie-theater, or some other public place. It should come as no surprise when many return and behave exactly the same way?

So what to do instead?

I learned this from my mentor and friend, Marcus Smith, a middle school Math teacher.

Mr. S.: I look forward to you following the rules we all agreed upon.

Student: So what happens if we don't follow them?

Mr. S.: Great question. I have no idea.

Student: What do you mean you have no idea?

Mr. S.: I have no idea. All situations will be looked at individually. Let's take fighting for example. If you decide to fight, probably there will be a consequence and probably it will be severe. But let's say that one of you totally started the fight and the other was just defending himself? One of you might get a five day suspension and the other might be commended for walking away. Also, I might even ask you the consequence you feel you deserve. That might be different from most teachers but that is how it is going to be in this room. Now do you see why I can't tell you in advance exactly what the

---

consequences will be. However, I trust I won't have to worry about that this year. I know you can follow the rules.

Making Traditional Consequences/Punishments Work Best:
Detention: There should always be instruction going on in the detention room, and no predetermined detention time. I prefer the teacher that assigns the detention do the instruction. This is done by staying with the student after school. For best results the teacher should begin by acknowledging his role in whatever happened. Then ask the student if there was anything she did wrong. For example:

Mr. M.: Richard, we got into it in class today, didn't we? Looking back at it, I know calling you out in front of your friends is not appropriate and I'm sorry. Sometimes I get emotional too and I don't mean to embarrass you. I'll try hard to control myself in the future even when you say things I don't like. Do you think there's anything you can do differently next time?

Student: Well I guess I don't have to call you a jerk.

Mr. M.: You guess? Because I said I am sorry. Guessing isn't good enough. What do you think you can do next time you get mad instead of calling me a name?

Student: Maybe I can just turn and walk away.

Mr. M.: So I will try hard not to embarrass you in front of your friends and if I do, you will try hard not to call me a name back. Good deal. Get out of here. Go home. I look forward to seeing you tomorrow.

The above is an example of how to model taking responsibility. The conversation might not go exactly this way, but I find when we admit our mistakes there is a much better chance students will take responsibility for their behavior. After the conversation send the student home. Keeping him there for the sake of misery turns this excellent conversation/consequence into a punishment.

In School Suspension:
    If you use In-School Suspension be sure students attend their academic classes. ISS should only be during classes the student likes. Be sure the ISS "teacher" is working with students on what they did wrong and what can be done differently in the future. It is very helpful if other teachers and administrators frequent the ISS room during the day. Some schools have their "coolest" teacher in the ISS room and students actually want to be there. If this is the case try to bring the ISS teacher into your classroom once a week to help teach a lesson or just be around the kids.

Call Suspended Students at Home:
    Try calling students who have been suspended from school that night at home. The specific conversation is given in the chapter on relationships on page 14. This is prevention. The goal is to set ourselves up for good behavior when she comes back. Remember, "Tough kids have tenure." They always come back.

Some Other Consequences:
    Now that we are no longer giving consequences in a predetermined sequence, it is possible to step outside the box and use non-traditional consequences. Remember, consequences are intended to teach better behavior. Punishments are intended to inflict

misery. Try to look for consequences that will improve the student, school, or community. Here are some examples:

1. You make a mess, you clean it up.
2. You do something destructive (i.e. fighting), you do something constructive (i.e. high school student works with elementary student).
3. Community Service (nursing homes and pet stores / humane society work well here).
4. Help the janitor clean classrooms or the cafeteria (Get parent permission first. Most will be happy to grant it).
5. Come to class late you stay as late as you came.

I Still Don't Know What to do:

Have you ever felt like you tried everything and still don't know what to do? I feel the same way sometimes. When this happens try telling the student how you are feeling and then ask what they would do if they were you. This is a conversation I had last year:

Mr. M: You know I am at my wits end with you. I will be honest. I feel like I have tried everything I know to get you to stop giggling and nothing seems to work. I guess I can continue to do the same silly ineffective things that we both know will not work. Or maybe you can tell me what I should do instead?

Jessica: Just move my seat. I giggle because I don't really have any friends. The two girls I sit by are nice to me so I feel like I need to impress them. If you just move my seat I promise I won't laugh anymore. If I do, I will serve the detention no questions asked.

I didn't move Jessica. Instead I moved the three around her and she never giggled again.

Move three for one:

Anytime you want to move a seat, I recommend moving three others as well. This eliminates the "you're always picking on me you never pick on anyone else" phrase. I didn't even move Jessica. I moved her two friends along with three others. This way it looked completely random.

Concluding Chapter Thought:

The word "insanity" is defined as doing the same thing over and over and expecting a different result. Can we agree that giving a student another detention after the first 66 haven't worked is crazy? There are times we need to be brave enough to try something else. The two most important things to remember about consequences are to teach a better way to behave, and to stop a behavior or action from happening again. Please do not have predetermined sequenced consequences for behaviors. Instead have "possible consequences" and add the word "other" to any school or classroom consequence list. This allows us to use anything on the list or something else that we think might be more effective.

CHAPTER EIGHT

Preventing Bullying

I recently received a call from a principal in Macon, GA to teach a seminar on bullying. She said it was a constant problem in their school and wondered if I would help get it to stop. Before I ever accept a seminar on bullying, I ask if they are really serious about dealing with the problem. Because if they are, schools and teachers need to make significant changes to the fundamental way they operate. Institutionalized events like rewards night, honor roll, class rankings, Fun Friday, and competitive grading systems, all contribute to the overall climate of students disliking each other.

Getting bullying to stop is obviously important and there are already books written on that. So I am not going to discuss intervention in this one. In my opinion, more important than getting bullying to stop is figuring out how to keep it from starting in the first place. Once it has started someone's feelings are already hurt. This chapter will focus on preventing bullying. How can we set up our classroom and school in a way that gets students to want to like and care about each other?

Good Intentions Don't Always Lead to Good Outcomes:

In a very innocent moment a teacher in Milwaukee looked at her class and said what thousands of us have actually been trained to do: catch kids being good. "When you are all sitting like Jennifer (she pointed to Jennifer) we will line up for lunch." Unwittingly, this teacher did something that causes bullying.

In another school, many miles from Macon and Milwaukee that I was visiting one week later, a teacher looked at his class and said, "I am so proud of Chris. He has been amazing this week. And because Chris has been so great he gets to pick any two people he wants for extended recess." This teacher just did something that causes bullying.

I walked into a 10th grade classroom recently in Florence, SC and heard this announcement by the principal over the loudspeaker. "Please excuse the following students for the National Honor Society Breakfast." This principal just did something that causes bullying.

In an 11th grade English class in Rochester, NY a student was complaining that her grade should be higher than a "B." The teacher responded by saying, "but your paper was not one of the best in the class so it is not an "A." This teacher just did something that can cause bullying.

I can go on and on. In fact, in almost every school I can point to specific things teachers and administrators do that cause kids to dislike each other. I will address each of the above incidents later in the chapter and show how with slight modifications they can go from helping cause bullying to getting students to care for each other. Before I do that here are nine systemic things teachers and schools can do that take guts and courage to help build a positive environment for your students.

Prevent Bullying: Do you have the courage to do the following?

• **Get rid of honor roll.** See, I knew you were not really serious about preventing bullying. Your smart kids already know they are smart. They don't need to be on a list for it. The low kids never get on the list and start resenting those who do. Honor roll serves no purpose in school other than to create a division among students. Some parents will complain at first. They'll get over it.

• **Grade students compared to their own previous work.** I remember my first day of 10th grade English in Mr. John's class. I looked around and saw Tori Smith, Alex Rios, and Christina Mann. I knew there was no chance of getting an "A" in that class. I was not nearly the writer they were and my reading skills have always been low. I remember Mr. John holding up Christina's paper saying, "This is an example of an 'A' in this class." At first I hated Mr. John, but he didn't really care. So I started hating Christina instead. It was easy for me to get others to hate her as well, since hardly anyone wrote like her and I was good at getting others to follow me. After all, I reasoned, it was her fault I couldn't get an "A" in that class.

Preventing this type of feeling among students is so easy, yet rarely done. Tell your students early in the school year that you will compare their work to their own previous work. Explain that you expect each to be a better writer today than they were yesterday.

I need you to read one more chapter today than you did yesterday. Yesterday you did 3 problems. Today it needs to be 5 or more. Approach behavior the same way. Yesterday in class you called out 6 times. Today it needs to be 3 or less. I'm sure you can count. Focus students on themselves and amazing things happen. Some will even ask their peers for help!

• **Eliminate class rankings:** When ranking a student first, we have to rank one last. Enough said? I have seen top students actually decide not to take advanced placement classes because they fear losing the higher ranking. Some students purposely give wrong answers to peers when asked for help. And please don't give me the "colleges need to know their ranking" argument. That's nonsense. There are schools in this country that have graduating classes of 400 and others with graduating classes of 40. Colleges look way beyond a class ranking to decide who they are going to select. If you absolutely must rank students, then do so, but don't tell students what they are ranked. After graduation, mail it home in a sealed envelope. I recently had a principal ask who would speak at graduation if they stopped ranking the students. At his school the valedictorian gave the speech. Schools that don't use rankings have seniors privately vote for the person they most want to hear from. After all, your best speakers are not always your best students!

• **Challenge the bully:** Most bullies are leaders. They have the ability to get others to follow them. I recall a situation that happened in my class a few years ago. Tony bullied Kyle, a mentally challenged senior. I approached Tony and said in a challenging tone, "You know, it is obvious you can get people to be mean to Kyle. We all see that. But if you were a real leader you would be able to get others to be nice to him. See it's easy for you and your friends to make fun of Kyle while he is eating alone. But are you capable of having him eat at your table with no one making fun of him? I guess we'll see." Within three days Kyle was eating at the table with Tony and his friends. In fact, Tony made sure no one made fun of Kyle again. Sometimes we need to teach the bully how to lead in a positive way. This takes real work, time, and effort. But I promise it is worth it!

• **Reward everyone in honor of one:** Pretend you are in fourth grade right now and the teacher says: "Hey everyone. I just want to let you know that Tom has been working really hard on his behavior this week and I am proud of him. Because he has been so good he gets two free nights of homework!" How do you feel about Tom? Most say, "Whatever with stupid Tom. What about me? I am good every week!" Instead, pretend the teacher says this: "Hey everyone, I just want to let you know that Tom has been working really hard on his behavior this week and I am really proud of him. Because Tom has been so good you all get an extra 2 free nights of homework in honor of Tom. Do not thank me. I had nothing to do with it. But if I were you I would thank Tom. He is the one who worked hard." Now how do you feel about Tom? Some will still dislike him. However, most are really excited because they are rewarded as well. Some might even say, "You better be good again next week!" We call this positive peer pressure and it is just as powerful as negative peer pressure. More on the difference between rewards and bribes later in the book.

• **Modify competitive games**: Two years ago I co-taught in a 10th grade Social Studies class. We decided to play "review jeopardy". Never again!

The class divided into two teams. Each member was required to answer a question correctly for his or her team to receive a point. Remember I said it was supposed to be review? Reviewing never happened. It was all about winning and losing instead of learning and reviewing. Later that day I overheard a girl on the losing team say to another student, "How did you not know that? It was so easy!" A solution is to give students that struggle two or three possible questions *and* the answers to those questions ahead of time. Now there is no panic when it is her turn, and true review can happen.

• **Use groups, but grade individually**: This way students work together on a project or presentation, but their grade is not contingent upon anyone else. If a group member is lazy or does not do his or her part there is no resentment from his peers. Resentment can lead to bullying. More on groups in chapter 12.

• **Avoid awards night or being a part of deciding who wins**: Just recently a colleague asked who I thought should win the English Writing Award. Everybody or nobody, I told him. He said they only had one award. My answer: Nobody. For me, one winner and 100 (give or take a few) losers are a bad ratio. And don't tell me parents like awards night. Most complain about their child not winning.

• **Create an "I am good at" board**: We wrote about this in one of our earlier books but this strategy is so valuable it needs to be explained again. Set aside a bulletin board with the name of each student on it. Under their own name each student writes one thing he is good at in school and one he is good at outside of school. If Kristy doesn't understand multiplication she can look at the "I'm good at board" and find someone to help her.

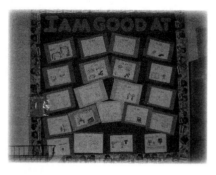

Students helping each other with things they are good at or enjoy goes a long way to prevent bullying. This strategy is also great if you get a new student during the school year. Before introducing the person to the class, have her look at the "I'm good at board" and pick out a few names she thinks she will be friends with.

For example, if Patricia is new and likes basketball, probably two or three others enjoy basketball as well. This strategy provides the teacher with a structured way to introduce Patricia to students who like basketball. Having something in common is so important for a new student.

Looking Back to Find a Better Way:

Now that you have some good prevention tools, let's look back at the earlier scenarios and see how the teachers mentioned were actually helping cause bullying:

In the first scenario the teacher innocently says, "When you are all sitting like Jennifer it will be time to go to lunch." The problem is many students don't care that Jennifer is sitting appropriately. In fact, after leaving the room some will call her names. Others will tease her for being the teacher's pet. It is almost never a good idea to single one student out in front of others. Jennifer might even decide not to sit so appropriately the next time just so she is not made the center of attention. Here is a different way for the teacher to say it without singling her out. "I'm glad to see some of you sitting appropriately. I appreciate it very much. Hopefully everyone else will be ready for lunch soon too."

In the second scenario the teacher publicly recognizes Chris for his outstanding behavior all week. Again, he is singled out. In this instance Chris is asked to pick any two people he wants for extended recess. The people he picks might be happy. However, those he does not pick get annoyed that they are left out. The teacher can easily solve this by giving the entire class extra recess time in honor of Chris. Now no one feels left out. Remember, rewarding everyone in honor of one is a great solution!

The same holds true for the next scenario. Instead of saying, "Please excuse the following students for the national honor society breakfast," the principal can say, "It is now time for the entire school to eat breakfast in honor of the national honor society students." All students get a chance to celebrate the achievements of a few by eating a special breakfast. If you want to put the honor society kids up at a special table, I'm relatively ok with that. But now everyone gets a bagel or a doughnut. Seems like a small price to pay for students liking each other. If you want to give the student an extra something just be sure to do it privately. The same modification can help make awards nights a more inclusive experience should your school decide against its elimination.

Sadly the last scenario is all too common. A student completes an assignment, is not happy with the grade, asks about it, and is told it is not as good as someone else's paper. This is easily avoided if we compare students to their own previous work. This strategy is not just for your low functioning students.

I greatly admire Tiger Woods. His press conference after a tournament is almost always the same. He wins by 10 shots and the reporter asks how he played. Tiger usually responds with some sort of, "I played ok." The reporter then says, "Ok? You won by 10 shots!" The reporter is comparing Tiger to everyone else. But Tiger is comparing himself to how he played the day before and the day before that. The only way to push students at the top is to compare their work to their own previous work. Without this type of grading system inclusion programs are sure to fail, and general education and special education students will dislike each other more than they already do.

When students ask why they received a certain grade on a paper, test, quiz, lab, etc... our answer should never have anything to do with any other student. As soon as it does we give students more reason to be annoyed with each other. Remember, be fair. Do not worry about treating everyone exactly the same way. Be sure graded work is given back face down. Do not have students peer edit unless it is a higher level class where all have strong self esteem.

Concluding Chapter Thought:

Learning cannot happen when students feel afraid, threatened and intimidated. The number one goal in every classroom to support learning should be building a close sense of community. I can't stand when kids pick on and make fun of each other. It is so important to do our best to try and prevent bullying. I am asking you to take a long honest look at your school and classroom policies to see if you are actually helping cause bullying. Do you compare students to each other? Do you publicly compliment one student while at the same time implying others are not doing as well as that person? Do you leave students out of activities, games, field trips, while others go? Do you ask students to choose one or two friends to "eat lunch with the teacher" or "spend extra time on the playground?" We cannot always control whether students pick on each other. However, it is our responsibility not to create an environment that promotes it.

CHAPTER NINE

Do you Reward or Bribe? Is there Really a Difference?

A re rewards good or bad? For the most part I believe rewards are good. If used correctly they can help teach kids to be responsible. Similarly, I believe bribes are mostly bad. Instead of teaching responsibility bribes often create spoiled kids expecting their next entitlement. Sadly, most teachers who think they are rewarding are actually bribing. Very few actually reward. Here is the difference: A reward only happens *after* a behavior. A bribe happens *before*. With a bribe the student knows he will get something. With a reward he does not know it is coming.

Here is an example of the difference between a reward and a bribe. Every Monday morning my students receive a "Bad attitude coupon." The coupon can be exchanged anytime during the week for three minutes of bad attitude time. Of course, there are some rules related to the coupon, most of which are about not bothering others.

Courtney, one of my most challenging students decides to use her coupon first thing Monday morning. A bribe is if I say this: "Ok Courtney, you can use your coupon now and if you are good the rest of the day you

---

get it back!" This is a bribe because the behavior has not happened yet. Any time we offer students something before they complete the behavior we are bribing. If Courtney wants the coupon back she might be good. But if she doesn't care about the coupon she probably won't. Either way, she is in charge. A reward is very different. When a student is rewarded she does not know it is coming, and the message is clearly sent that if she ever asks the answer will be no.

Courtney uses her coupon early Monday morning. A reward would be:

"Courtney, I just want to tell you I am really proud of how you behaved today. You used your coupon first thing this morning and I know it was hard for you to be good the rest of the day. Great job. I look forward to another awesome day tomorrow."

Seventy percent of the time it ends there. Thanks. Good job. Way to go. No ticket, sticker, point, etc... However, thirty percent of the time is different:

"Courtney, I just want to let you know I am really proud of how you behaved today. You used your coupon first thing this morning and I know it was hard for you to behave the rest of the day. Nice job today. I look forward to another great day tomorrow. By the way, here is your coupon back. Feel free to use it again this week if you want. And Courtney, I know you will never ask for the coupon back, right? Because if you ever ask the answer will always be?..." She will fill in the *"No"* for you. *"But great job today. I can't wait to see you again tomorrow!"*

This is a reward because the behavior already happened and I decided to give her the coupon back. She did not behave just to get the coupon. But knowing she might get it is an incentive, and sometimes students need incentives.

Here are a few other common examples of bribes:
"If you are good all day we'll have 30 minutes of recess time at the end of the day."

"If you do your homework you'll get a sticker."

"If we all behave this week there will be a pizza party on Friday."

"We are going to have Fun Friday every Friday afternoon. If you behave all week you will get to participate!"

"When you finish that work you can go on the computer!"

Turning these bribes into rewards:
"Hey class, I expect you to behave all day. Sometimes when you do there will be extra recess time at the end of the day and sometimes there will not. But if you ask for extra recess time I reserve the right to say no. So please do not ask (30% of the time you must give extra recess time)."

"Sometimes I will give stickers for doing a great job on your homework and sometimes I will not. But if you start asking for stickers... ."

"On most Friday afternoons we will do something really fun. If you misbehave during the week you might not be able to attend. I look forward to you behaving."

"Finishing your work is important, and after it is complete you might be allowed to go on the computer. However, please do not ask to use the computer. If you ask I will probably say no."

Don't be scared by the *"I will probably say no"* part. If you say yes the student is actually surprised and feels really good about you!

Reward Everyone in Honor of One:
I wrote about this in the bullying chapter. Reward your entire class or your entire school in honor of a student or a group of students. This is a great way to build a classroom or school community. It is also how you can include a particular student who is always in trouble. Right before "Fun Friday" or a field trip, tell the student that is not allowed to participate that they are now allowed. In a not so nice tone of voice say this, *"I still am not happy with you, but because Erica has behaved so well this week, even you (the student left out) get to go too. It is all because of Erica. It has nothing to do with me. I'm still not happy with you!"* Now no one is left out. Sometimes I might pick two students that do not like each other and set up a scenario where one gets rewarded in honor of the other. I have watched students that can't stand each other become instant friends because of this strategy.

Almost Never Punish Everyone Because of One:
Punishing the entire class because of one student is not usually a good idea. It often gets everyone mad at one and takes away from the classroom community we are trying to build.

What if I want to give an individual student something extra?

Be sure to do it privately. No announcements or big scenes in front of the whole class. So it goes like this: *"Because Erica has been so well behaved this week you all get an extra 15 minutes on the playground in honor of her. Do not thank me, thank her."* When everyone else is on the playground simply pull Erica aside privately and say this: *"By the way, here is a free homework pass just for you. I will not be discussing this with anyone else."* And then walk away. Get out of there. With this new outlook on rewards we can give something extra although we are not obliged to. Either way, we make the decision!

So do you ever leave students out? Does everyone always gets recess, etc...?

Sometimes a student needs to be kept out of recess or excluded from a field trip. Just be sure to weigh the long term effects of doing this. Will the exclusion teach the student anything about better behavior? Is potentially building more resentment, hostility, and anger worth it? Sometimes the answer is yes because the student needs to understand that he must work at changing his behavior and in life certain privileges must be earned. This is why it is so important not to predetermine consequences and not to threaten certain actions. Once we threaten we must follow through.

What do I think of stickers?

It is not about the stickers, it is about how they are given. There is nothing worse than having a student finish his work and say, "but last year we got a sticker when we did that!" If you are going to give stickers try giving everyone a sticker in honor of one. Then at the end of the day give the honored student an extra sticker privately. Please do not have a sticker chart or board in the room. Tell your class to have their own sticker chart at home.

My Sticker Detox Program:
When I worked in a 4th grade room one recent summer, I started a "detoxification" program because trust me, they were addicted.

Mr. M.: *Ok. I think I just heard someone say they want a sticker. I'm hoping I didn't hear that. Stickers you guys, are for little kids, like 3rd graders. They are NOT cool anymore. Some will be disappointed. But there will always be one student who never got a sticker in his life. He will yell, "yeah, stickers are dumb." Now you have the whole class. By the way, if I taught 3rd grade I would have said, stickers are for second graders... And if I taught 2nd grade I would have said they were for first graders... If I taught kindergarten I wouldn't have given cigarettes (just kidding), I mean stickers in the first place. But once you start smoking it's hard to stop!*

Why does bribing create spoiled kids?
At the end of lunch an exasperated seminar participant said she just called back to school and her class was totally out of control. She was a huge briber! Bribing will get good behavior in the presence of adults or authority. But now this teacher is at a staff development day, her sub doesn't know the bribing system, and students are out of control. Good behavior in the presence of authority should never be enough.

Adults are not on the bus, in the cafeteria, or in the locker room. The goal is for students to behave whether we are there or not. When students learn that they get things for certain behaviors, some will manipulate situations to be seen doing those things. I recall watching a student intentionally drop trash on the ground. He stood near the trash until the teacher turned around, and then said "Look Ms. Smith, I'm picking this up and I didn't even drop it!" Ms. Smith gave him a ticket. I was disgusted.

Bribing is Better than Chaos:

Some teachers believe bribes work because they can change behavior quickly. So if you have total chaos, then bribe. But this should never be enough. We want students to behave because it is the right thing to do. And in the real world sometimes you get something for doing the right thing and sometimes you don't. So that's how it should work in the classroom.

Concluding Chapter Thought:

Two months ago I walked into a faculty meeting. Our principal began by saying to the entire staff, "Thank you so much for the extra work many of you are putting in. Janet, I know you have been staying after school to help struggling readers. Kris, I saw you pick up a piece of paper you didn't drop. Thanks. Tom and Jeff, the music concert was excellent. Thanks to all of you for doing such a great job. As a faculty you all have been amazing. Thanks." That was it. There were no stickers, tickets, points, or raffles. And believe me, a well deserved "thanks" was all we needed. This is how most faculty meetings went.

Two months later I walked into a faculty meeting

to a table full of food. Our principal said, "The food is for all of you. I appreciate how hard you have been working this month. Thanks for all you do." This is how to reward. Almost always the only thing students need is a heartfelt "thanks, good job, I noticed." Once in a while it is nice to give everyone a little something extra without telling them ahead of time.

CHAPTER TEN

What is "Challenge?"
Using Challenge to Motivate and Manage

Almost everyone likes a challenge as long as they believe the challenge can be successfully accomplished. If the ability to succeed is not there (no matter how many stickers you give I still can't read it!), challenge will only lead to annoyance and frustration. When challenging a student we are basically saying, "I am not sure you have the ability to succeed. I guess we will see." Realize this only works if a student really does have the ability. Here is an example of how to use challenge to get students to behave better when you are gone (i.e. for a substitute). Say this to the entire class:

"Hey guys. I just want to let you know that I will not be here tomorrow. I am taking the day off to attend a workshop. I want to let you all know right now that I trust you will behave when I am gone. I look forward to a great report when I get back."

Then as they are walking out of the room pull the leaders aside and say this:

"Hey real quick. You know what I just said to the entire class about them behaving tomorrow when I'm gone? Well, actually I lied. I don't care how they behave. I really don't. You see, the only two names I

am looking at when I get back are the two of you. You guys are able to get everyone to follow you all the time. Of course, we all know you can lead them in a negative way. But I'm not so sure you can lead in a positive way. I don't know if you have the ability to help get everyone quiet. I guess we'll see. I don't know if you really have the ability to help get everyone lined up for lunch. I guess we'll see that too. I look forward to reading the report when I get back."

I'm not saying this approach will always get them to behave, or help influence others to behave. However, many students will do the right thing just to prove you wrong. And when it happens do not get excited. Instead say,

"Well yeah I am proud of what you were able to do when I was gone, and thanks for helping influence others. But seriously, anyone can behave and lead in a positive way for one day. I would be really impressed if it happened for a full week."

Are you getting this? Then after a week it is:

"Who can't behave for a week? I will be really proud and excited after a full month. But I am not so sure you are capable of that. I guess we will see."

Adopt these "Challenge" Phrases:
- *Yesterday you did 3 problems. That's good. I'm not so sure you can do all 5 tonight though. I guess we will see.*
- *Great job with your reading homework. But I don't think there is any chance you will complete it two nights in a row! Good luck though!*
- *I know you behaved today and that really is great. But I would be much more impressed if*

you acted the same way tomorrow. I am not sure you have it in you. Good luck!

- *I am not so sure you even have the ability to lower your voice. Do you?*
- *You did a really good job behaving on the field trip. And I am proud. But do you think you are able to behave that way on the next field trip?*

Because I am not so sure. I guess we will see. I hope you are able to see why challenge works so well. Difficult kids are constantly threatened about what will happen if they don't do certain things. For the most part it makes them mad and their goal becomes to show the teacher they will do whatever they please.

Should we ever be sarcastic with kids?
Yes. I know I know. Every educational expert tells us never to be sarcastic with kids. In fact, I attended a workshop with a very famous behavior expert. He said we should never be sarcastic with kids because "sarcasm leaves a scar that will never heal." What he should have said is, "When used incorrectly and the student does not get it, sarcasm leaves a scar that will never heal." To me, sarcasm is like a relatively dangerous chemical that might be used in chemistry class. If you do not know what to do with the chemical stay away from it! But does that mean nobody should ever use it? Some teachers that have strong relationships with students are good at using sarcasm. My rule is this: I need to be 100% sure a student knows I am being sarcastic. Be sure you have a strong relationship with the student and almost never use sarcasm with a student in front of his peers. Sarcasm only works when the student knows we are being sarcastic! That's the whole point.

Concluding Chapter Thought:

The key to a good challenge is for the person being challenged to have the ability to meet and succeed at whatever the challenge is. If the challenge is impossible or cannot be met we leave the person feeling frustrated and angry. After a student meets a challenge, you might celebrate the accomplishment but more important is to use it as a springboard to fulfilling the next challenge. For example, "Yes, you did do a nice job on the homework problems, and you should feel pleased with the effort you put in. I wonder if you have it in you to make it two days in a row. I am not so sure but I guess we'll see tomorrow. Good luck."

CHAPTER ELEVEN

Groups and Transitions:
Common times students disrupt and what to do

The effectiveness of many instructional moments depends upon how well students can work together. This is especially true during cooperative learning activities. Some students believe that the word "group" is a license to disrupt. When groups are well-organized, there is often no better form of learning. However, kids often use this time to catch up on the latest television shows, sporting events and gossip. There are a few essential ingredients to ensure smoothly run groups inside the classroom. When assigning students to work in groups, the following guidelines can be most helpful:

- **Groups should have no more than five members.** Four is ideal, but we can live with five. Six or more is a recipe for group disaster.

- **Each member of the group should have a specific role.** We suggest numbering each member of the group 1-5. Then give each a task. For example, number ones are the group leader. Their only job is

---

to make sure everyone else is doing his or her job. Number twos are the readers. Threes are the note takers. Fours are the writers. Number fives are the group presenters. Of course, create any categories that fit your specific class or lesson.

- **Change up roles?** Not always. The Yankees do not put their starting shortstop at catcher just to "change it up." Try putting students in positions where they are best. Some are natural leaders. Others are better at reading. This is not the time for me to teach a student how to read. The only role I require is "presenter." This is because students rarely practice public speaking in school.

- **Give specific instructions.**
  Once groups are seated and quiet we can give specific instructions for each member. I like to make it the group leader's responsibility to help get his or her group focused and paying attention. Group leaders need to write down the instructions for all members. Each member only writes down his specific role.

- **It is always easier to extend than it is to take away**. Figure out how much time the activity is going to take. Then cut it in half. For example, if I believe an activity will take 10 minutes, I tell students they have five. By giving less time we create a sense of urgency, and there is a greater likelihood they will get right to work. If students are working well and five minutes pass I can extend another few minutes without anyone knowing. By contrast, try taking time away, and someone always complains.

- **Bring groups back but allow slower groups to finish.**
It is common to hear someone say, "but we aren't finished yet." It is important that we extend the time if most groups are not finished. However, if it is just one or two, allow them to finish while beginning the next thing with everyone else. This way the finished groups are not bored while waiting for slower groups.

- **Red Cup - Yellow Cup - Green Cup.** Give each group leader a red, yellow, and green plastic cup. If the leader concludes that the group needs help that will take more than a quick explanation, he puts the red cup in front. Yellow means the group has a quick question that needs a quick answer. When green is visible, it means all is okay. This allows us to avoid being the annoying teacher that constantly asks students if everything is ok. It also gives the teacher a few minutes of chill time.

- **Only talk to the leader.** Say this to the class: Hey class, just so you know, during group time there are only 6 people in this room that are allowed to talk to me. If you are not a group leader I do not want to hear from you. You go to your group leader. If they can't help they will come to me." Now instead of managing 30 students, we only have to pay attention to 6 leaders. Like captains on a football or soccer team who take charge on the field, group leaders allow us to manage a large group while focusing and dealing with only a few. This is how we get students working for us.

Tips for Managing Transitions:

Last night I was watching television. The show ended at 10pm and before I could shut it off a voice came on that said, "The next episode of Law and Order begins right now!" And then boom, Law and Order was on and I was watching. By the time the first break came, about five minutes in, I was hooked. I rushed to the bathroom and hurried back so I wouldn't miss the next segment.

Television has mastered the art of transition. It used to be that a show ended, credits rolled, a long commercial break followed, and then the next show began. Not anymore. Television stations know that once they lose a viewer, it is very hard to get that person back.

So how does this relate to teaching? Transitioning from one subject to another or from one activity to another can be a huge source of disruption. Teachers often tell me their class behaves so well during an activity, but once they are asked to transition from Math to English, or English to Science, or from a group activity to seat work, it becomes a free-for-all. The problem is that many teachers stop teaching during the transition. For example, I often hear this, "Ok guys we are finished with English and you did a great job. I'll give you 3 minutes and then we are starting Science. I'll wait." This is not the way. Law and Order does not wait. It begins, right now! Teachers should not wait either. Teach right through the transition. Say this, "You have three minutes to return to your seats for Science, and while you are returning watch the demonstration I am doing. So walk and look at the same time." I do this naturally in my seminar. I often do an activity where people work with partners. They are usually with someone on the opposite side of the room. When the activity is finished I instruct them back to their seats by saying, "As you are walking back to your seats I am going to share my favorite strategy of the day." This is known as a tease, and most rush back to write it down. In a real classroom, teaching through transitions will greatly limit disruption. Then five minutes into the new activity I can take a break, if needed.

Concluding Chapter Thought:

To make groups work best, be sure to give each student a role and tell how long the task is going to take before instructing them on what to do. Let students know the only ones allowed to talk to the teacher are the group leaders. If any other member of the group is struggling they need to go to the group leader first. The only time I allow students to decide their group partners is when I do not mind them working with friends. Instead of placing friends together say, "Today I am going to be nice and allow you decide who you would like to work with. So now you can't say I never let you pick your partners!" If there is a student that is chronically left out, privately ask a couple of students to invite that person to be in their group.

CHAPTER TWELVE

What is Causing the Behavior?
Basic needs we all have

We can almost always trace inappropriate behavior to the non-fulfillment of one of three basic needs. Think of these needs as three separate pipes that can either be filled with water or dry. When full, think of the student as "hydrated" which usually leads to well behaved, hard working, kids who participate in class and rarely disrupt. However, when the hydration system is dry it is almost a guarantee they will disrupt. The good thing for teachers is that only one of the pipes needs to be filled for good behavior. If all three are filled we have an outstanding student. The problem for many students is that all three pipes are dry. Each pipe is described below along with specific ideas for filling the hydration system. Remember, when a person is totally dehydrated they are not immediately flooded with liquids. The liquids are given slowly. The same holds true here. Slowly you can implement these strategies to begin the hydration process and improve behavior.

Need 1...The Feeling of Power and Control:

Do you always like someone telling you what to do? Most students don't either. Schools are not set up for kids to feel any power or control. In fact, there are almost no places for students to make legitimate decisions. Think about it. We tell them everything: the homework, rules, consequences, what time to eat, how to dress, if they are allowed to go to the bathroom, if they can get a drink, what their schedule is, what the test is going to look like, what is on the test... I could go on.

When someone is constantly told what to do and how to do it they will often rebel against the authority just to show they can. Most students have other places in their lives where the power/control need is fulfilled, which is why they do not disrupt. They might be the captain of a team, play an instrument, or get to make decisions at home. But a small percentage of students have no power or control in any part of their lives. It is very important for teachers to set clear, firm guidelines and limits. But within these limits students need to have a say to fulfill this need. Here are a bunch of different ways to make students feel like they have some power and control, while still maintaining firm limits:

Dress Code or Uniforms:

Imagine if your boss tells you it is very important to dress up for work. No big deal, right? Now imagine she says, "this means you will wear a white button up shirt, black dress pants, a black belt, black socks, and black shoes. By the way, no cologne or perfume please. And those shoes need to be thoroughly polished every day." Get the point? Originally we are ok with being told to dress up. But the extreme managing of every detail becomes annoying. Teachers know not to wear a bathing suit and tank top to work. But within the parameters of dressing up, it is nice for us to have some choices. Does it really matter if I wear a blue shirt or a white shirt? Is it a big deal if I wear brown shoes or black? Kids are no different.

Adults can create the parameters for a dress code, such as all students will wear a button up shirt and khaki colored pants. However, allow students to decide which button up shirt they want to wear. If your school requires uniforms I suggest creating four different options. Then allow students to decide which they want to wear and on which days.

Here are more examples of how to give choices while setting limits so students feel more in control:

Limit: Calling me inappropriate names is not ok.
Choice: What do you propose happens so you remember not to use language like this again?

Limit: Writing is very important and I need to know that you understand what a paragraph is.
Choice: So quickly decide which essay question out of these three you want to answer.

Limit: Reading is critical to success in life and I need to know you are improving.
Choice: Here are five books. Read all of the back covers and decide which book is best for you to read.

Think of the limit as a boundary. Have you every played baseball or softball? The rule is that the hitter has to be inside the batters box. However, each hitter is allowed to decide where they want to stand within the box. Some might move up for a curve ball or off speed pitcher, but then stand as far back as possible when facing a fastball pitcher. Think of choices the same way in a classroom. The amount of problems can be the box. Which problems the student chooses is the movement inside the box.

Take a Shot!

If a student does not agree with a decision I make he can "take a shot" at changing my mind. He must make an appointment to see me at a time when nobody else is around. He then gets two uninterrupted minutes to convince me that I: should give a higher grade, not call his mom, let him go on the field trip, participate in Fun Friday, etc... It is a good idea for the student to set a timer. When finished we separately write a "Y" (yes you convinced me) or "N" (no you didn't) on a piece of paper and compare. Students are usually honest when grading their performance.

The goal is for students to practice the skill of convincing which fulfills the need for power and control. Sales people and lawyers spend a lot of time doing this. Students that are successful usually spend a lot of time planning their argument and think through what they are going to say. I also allow students to take their shot on paper if they prefer writing to speaking. Remember, a lack of power and control is often at the root of disruptive behavior. Take a few minutes to brainstorm how many times during a day you make a decision that can be made just as easily by your students.

Need 2...Competence:

I recently heard a teacher say, "All kids are good at something!" True. But do all believe they are good at something? Most people feel competent somewhere in their life. It might be on a basketball court, soccer field, or in a concert hall. She might be great in the art room, church youth group, or dance class. Others are good at school. They sit still, pay attention, memorize facts, get good grades, and fit in socially. But occasionally a student is not involved in anything outside of school, is not good academically, and struggles socially. For this student a feeling of competence is critical to improved success in school, and for good long term behavior.

Pretend right now you only have two options for the rest of the day. You are going to get a big stamp on your forehead that says "BAD" or "STUPID". Which will you pick? Some students see these as their only two options. They already fail every test and are missing nine homework assignments. At least acting bad takes attention away from feeling stupid. Many specific strategies already described earlier in the book make students feel competent. These are listed below but not explained. Anything with an explanation is new.

• **Get it right.** There is nothing better for a student with low self esteem than getting a problem correct in front of his peers. There is nothing worse than getting it wrong. Say this to a student: "Tonight for homework I want you to do number 7 and just number 7. Tomorrow in class you will do number 7 on the board in front of everyone. When you finish tonight be sure to check your answer against mine (yes, give the answer) just to be sure it is correct." Tomorrow the student comes to class and gets the problem right. Now he starts to feel good about math. The next night "the homework is number 16 and 24. Check number 16 against mine but do 24 on your own. Sound good? Get here early so I can look at both of them. If number 24 is wrong, don't worry, you will only do 16 on the board." Slowly but surely his attitude about math will change!

• **Mistake of the Day.** My friend Kerry has a mistake of the day. First she gets permission from a student who made a mistake. Then she holds up the mistake a student makes and explains how good the error is. She says, "I can totally understand how it is possible to make this mistake. In fact, some of the rest of you made the same mistake. So good job. By the way, here is how to fix it."

• **Compare kids to their own work.**

• **Open book / Open note tests and quizzes.**

• **Use private signals when correcting a student.**

Need 3...Belonging:

The final basic need is to belong. Everyone wants to feel like an important and valued member of whatever he or she is doing. Many students do not feel like they belong in school. Some teachers perpetuate this belief by kicking them out and getting frustrated when they return. Here are some strategies to make students feel as if they belong. Again, if mentioned previously I do not explain it here.

• **Tell them you care.** I challenge you to take one minute every day to say the following to a challenging (or non-challenging) student: "I know we argue a lot and sometimes it might even seem like I don't want you here. But you are important and overall I like having you in my class. Thanks for coming every day." We all like to feel cared about. Be sure to tell students every day.

- **Introduce students to each other.** It is important to quickly assess the likes, strengths, and dislikes of students. Then I try to introduce students to each other that you believe will be friends. Sometimes we can even introduce their parents as well. Remember the "I am good at board" can be a big help for this.

- **Emphasize strengths.** Is someone a bad reader but a great speaker? Is someone else a horrible listener but great leader? Sometimes it is hard to find student strengths. Emphasize them and set up situations in class for students to utilize what they are good at.

- **Specific class jobs.**

- **Involvement in clubs, sports, activities...** Including being on the team or a manager.

Here are a few other reasons students misbehave:

- **Awareness.** This is rare but does occasionally happen. Awareness means the student is literally not aware of the behavior. Some students with ADHD fall into this category. The student that taps her pen non-stop sometimes is unaware of what she is doing. I have shared numerous strategies (carpet on the desks, music stands) for students with awareness issues.

• **Attention**. Some students are desperate for attention. There are two completely different reasons some are desperate for attention.

Student "A" gets complete undivided attention at home. He is often an only child, which allows 100% of adult attention to be focused on him. He has not learned how to share, wait his turn, and follow rules. All of a sudden this student is dropped in an environment with 20 others. For him it can be hard to cope. The lack of attention when you are one of 20 then leads to disruptive behavior so the focus turns back to him.

Student "B" often gets zero attention anywhere else in her life. She too is desperate for someone to notice her and often will act out because in her mind negative attention is better than no attention. She might have 4 or 5 siblings at home and her accomplishments, successes, and failures, often go unnoticed at home. She will seek attention from somewhere, and disrupting class almost always gets noticed.

Remember, these are two very different students and working with them will require different approaches. Student "A" needs clearly defined limits that allow for choice within those limits. For example, "you can be on the computer for 15 minutes. Would you prefer those minutes at the beginning, middle, or end of class?" The choice takes the focus off the limit (15 minutes). He begins to learn he does not get whatever he wants for as long as he wants it. He is then praised (privately) when after 15 minutes he gets off the computer without being told. This shifts the attention to him in a positive way.

Student "B" needs to be privately praised as well. Be sure to reassure her on a daily basis that she is doing a good job and that you are proud of her.

Private conversation explaining that it must be hard to not get a lot of attention at home can be helpful as well. Do not be afraid to discuss personal issues with this student. Showing her you understand her as well as she understands herself can go a long way in changing behavior.

- **Need to look *"cool"* in front of their friends.** If others are watching you can expect certain students to challenge your authority. Kids need to look cool in front of each other. Let them. The second to last word is almost always best. Remember that anytime you want to deliver a message to a student and others can hear, there is a good chance a power struggle will ensue.

Concluding Chapter Thought:

It is important to understand why a student is misbehaving before we can figure out exactly what "medicine" to give. Taking some time to diagnose the problem makes fixing it easier. For example, the best way to address the need for power and control in the classroom is to offer your students choices within non-negotiable limits. Remember, the hitter has to be inside the batter's box. However, each hitter is allowed to decide where they want to stand within the box. Some move up for a curve ball or off speed pitch, but stand as far back as possible when facing a fastball pitcher. The "limit" or "batters box" should not be negotiable. A student showing me he knows how to multiply is the batter's box. The amount of problems it takes to show me this might be up to him.

CHAPTER THIRTEEN

Power Stuggles:
How to diffuse them

Power Struggles always happen for the same reason. The student does not want to look bad in front of the class and neither does the teacher. Here is an example of a power struggle I watched between a 10 year old girl in Tulsa and her teacher. This happened in the hallway in front of the entire class.

Teacher: Maliqua, I saw you drop that piece of paper. Pick it up now.
Maliqua: No. I didn't drop it.
Teacher: Yes you did, I saw you. You have five seconds to pick it up. 5, 4, 3...
Tina (Maliqua's friend): Can I just pick it up for her?
Teacher: No! You didn't drop it. Maliqua, let's go! You are holding us up.
Maliqua: I didn't drop it and I'm not picking it up. You can count all day for all I care.
Teacher: Then you need to go down to the office.
Maliqua: You can't make me and I ain't going.
Teacher: Fine, then I'll call down to the office and they will come get you.

Maliqua: You think I care? Go ahead, bitch.
Teacher: What did you call me?
Maliqua: You heard me.
Teacher: That's it. You're gone.

Maliqua ended up with a two day suspension for "insubordination." A two day suspension that began over the issue of dropping a piece of paper! Unfortunately, this is not uncommon in many classrooms. Often a minor disagreement or argument turns into a much bigger issue. Fortunately this can easily be diffused by a teacher with a few easy to learn skills.

These are my Goals when a Power Struggle Happens:

Try to keep students in class. If a student is not here he cannot be listening. If he is not listening, he cannot be learning, and if he is not learning how can he pass a state exam? If he fails a state exam some people might think you are a bad teacher. So he needs to be here.

Get back to teaching. After delivering a private message to a student it is best to walk away. As you walk the student will mumble under her breath. Keep teaching. Do not go back!

There are 8 Major Steps to Diffusing any Student:

Become a 2nd to last word person. Did you know teachers were born "last word type people?" Think about your own personal life. I bet you always need to have the last word. When I finally allowed myself to become a second to last word person I was able to get out of almost any argument or any power struggle with any student. Understand that students will mumble a few inappropriate things under their breath as we are walking away. Keep walking. Remember, second to last word is almost always best! By the way, my last word is almost always, "Thanks." "I think I saw you drop that piece of paper and I'd appreciate if you picked it up! Thanks." Then get out of there!

Get out of there! So many teachers send a message and then stick around for a response. Stop sticking around. Say what you need to say and move. Power struggles can't happen if the teacher is not there. Remember, it is easier to walk away when you have trained yourself to be a second to last word person.

Recognize the battle is about to happen. Pay close attention to the student you are talking to. Does he like to argue? Does a discussion with him often lead to a power struggle? If you recognize a back and forth argument, try the four w's of diffusing. These four steps will almost always get the argument to end.

"**Whoa!**" (as loud as I can to get their attention).

What (Let the student know what is happening). "You and I are about to argue right now."

Why (It's always the same reason). "You don't want to look bad in front of your friends and neither do I."

When (Do not leave him hanging!). "So let's talk about it right after class, thanks." And then move. Get out of there. Do not stick around for a response!

Notice I do not tell the student it is his fault. "You and I are about to argue right now. You don't want to look bad in front of your friends and neither do I." Again I do not blame the student. "So let's talk about it right after class." The last line is so important because no one likes being left hanging. Give a specific time to discuss the issue. Most students will not stay to talk after class. However, a few will and if they do we better listen. They are taking their own time to talk to us. It must be important.

Use humor. The introduction of this book gives two examples of diffusing by using humor. I am not asking you to become a clown and remember, there should often if not always be consequences given at a later time. But in the moment, diffusing by using humor often leaves the student speechless.

Steps 5-8 are Our Award Winning 4 Step Process of Diffusing (Mendler, A. 1997):

> **Listen** (hear what the student is saying, not how he is saying it).
>
> **Acknowledge** (let the student know you hear him).

Agree (let them know that what they are saying is or might me true).

Defer (we will discuss this at a later time).

It goes like this:
Andy: Mr. Mendler, this lesson sucks!
Mr. Mendler: Andy, I hear you. (listen and acknowledge).

Now the hardest part. Agree. Let the student know that what he is saying is or might be true.
Andy: Mr. Mendler, this lesson sucks!
Mr. M: Andy I hear you and I have to say you might be right.

This is so hard because we usually do not want to agree! But there is no better way to diffuse any human being than to agree with what they are saying. The final step is to defer to a later time when you are available to discuss.
Andy: Mr. Mendler, this lesson sucks.
Mr. M: Andy. I hear you and I have to say you might be right. But right now is not the time to talk about it. I promise right after class. Thanks for waiting.

And then get out of there! Move. Do not stick around and quickly get back to the lesson Andy interrupted.

What if it continues? Is removal ever an option?

Yes. But try hard not to remove a student during the first month of the school year. Sometimes things get so out of control that teaching is impossible or safety is an issue. Those are the parameters for student removal. If and when this happens the conversation looks like this.

Mr. M (as privately as possible): You know what? Your behavior is so rude and so out of control that I can't teach anymore. Do you see the door over there? Look! If you need to leave feel free and go. I would prefer that you stay and behave yourself because you are an important part of our class and I will miss you when you are gone. But go if you need to go, come back as soon as you are ready to learn. I hope that is very soon.

Let me break this down. First a limit is set. "Your behavior is rude and out of control that I can't teach." Then the door is pointed out. Some will look and some will not. It doesn't matter. Notice the student is offered the door. This is very different from kicking her out. She is also told it is preferred that she stay and behave. This is the truth. Remember, keeping kids in class is always the first goal. The next two lines are very important. "You are an important part of our class and I'll miss you when you're gone (sometimes this is hard to say because deep down we do not feel like we will miss that student when he is gone. But I recommend fighting through that and saying it anyway)." Now if her mom calls and asks why she was kicked out I have a good response. Not only did I not kick her out, but I told her I would prefer she stay. I also said she is an important part of our class, and that I will miss her when she is gone. That is hardly kicking her out. Notice the last line. "Please come back as soon as you are ready to learn." Say the last line because she will come back. They always do.

Here is the math on this. With this approach 50%

of the time she leaves and 50% of the time she stays. If she leaves follow whatever your school requires for student removal. But now you have at least prevented an administrator or parent from asking why she was kicked out. Of those that stay, 50% of the time they stay and behave. This means 25% of the time this approach works with extremely disruptive students. Twenty-five percent of the time they stay and continue to disrupt. If this happens I simply do what many of you would have done before reading this book. "Get out!" I can still go there. It is just so important to try hard not to.

Concluding Chapter Thought:

Being tough should mean making it tough for students to throw away their education. Every time a student gets kicked out, not only has he become someone else's problem, but he has also succeeded in throwing his education away for that day. Yes there are times teaching is made so difficult that removal must happen. But there are many things we can do in the classroom that take very little time to effectively diffuse a disruptive student, keep him in class and get back to teaching.

CONCLUSION

The Teacher That Changed My Life:

I got into a lot of trouble in school. In fact, I was kicked out/removed from public school in 6th grade. It happened in the middle of the year. I was at my new school for two weeks when I was summoned to Mr. D's room. Mr. D. was a 7th grade English teacher. I remember walking into his room. The lights were off and he was leaned back in his chair with his feet up on the desk. Mr. D. was an older gentleman with gray spiked hair. He always wore a big fat bow tie and a cardigan sweater. There was a row of windows on top of the wall and light poured into the room. Mr. D. was reading the paper and barely acknowledged me as I walked in. I sat down and waited for him to say something. It seemed like we had been sitting in silence for an eternity. In reality, it was about 3 minutes.

Finally Mr. D. slid his chair close to mine. He looked directly into my eyes and said, "Brian I just want to tell you something."

Now you have to understand I was always prepared for an argument. I was ready. Mr. D. then said, "I just want to tell you... that I love having you in my class." For the first time in my school life I was

---

speechless. It took thirteen years for a teacher to tell me they liked having me in class. Everyone else spent their time figuring out how to get rid of me. Do you know there is a student right now in your class who does not believe you like him? I challenge you to walk in tomorrow and tell that student you love teaching him. It goes a long way.

I looked at Mr. D. and said "what?" He said, "I love teaching kids like you. Two weeks ago this school was boring and now it is fun." For the first time a teacher complimented me. He said, "Do you see that world out there?" He pointed outside and looked at the same time. "Yes. I see it," I told him. "Brian, just so you know, you are going to be wildly successful in that world. You are smart, funny, and you know how to tell a great story. You are a heck of a speaker, too. That world loves people like you. But unfortunately you are going to struggle in school."

I sat there and listened. Mr. D. continued, "You see Bri, schools have already created a mold of what a student is supposed to look like. Sit still, do what you're told, listen, pay attention, raise your hand, etc... Unfortunately you don't fit the mold. And when you don't fit they try to jam you in or get you out. And Bri, you don't fit."

He continued by asking a question. Mr. D. was a great question asker. "Do you mind if I help you? Do you mind if I help you get better at being who you already are? You see Bri, I know you love comedy and jokes, and storytelling. So from now on you get the first five minutes of class or three jokes, whichever comes first." I said, "You're gonna let me tell jokes? And I'm not even going to get in trouble for it?" He said, "Of course you're not going to get in trouble. I love jokes. I just don't like them all class long. So pick the three best each day. You start tomorrow. Ok. You can leave." As I was walking toward the door Mr. D. said, "Bri, if you stink, we can boo. Kind of like in a real comedy club. Okay?" I smiled and couldn't wait to get home. I'll never forget walking into my house that afternoon. I was so excited. I remember saying, "Mom, I got this English teacher that's gonna let me tell jokes in class tomorrow! He says I have a real skill and he is going to work on it with me." My mom didn't quite believe me so she called him. I'll never forget that conversation. My mother had been involved in many conversations with many teachers. Theirs went like this.

Mrs. M: Hi Mr. D.? It's Mrs. Mendler, Brian's mom.

Mr. D.: (cutting her off): Oh yeah. I love teaching Brian. I'm so glad he came to this school. Mrs. Mendler, your son is very smart. He has a ton of energy. He is obviously a leader and his speaking skills are amazing!

Mrs. M.: Wow. Thanks for saying all that. Brian says you are going to let him tell jokes in class. Is that true?

Mr. D.: Yes ma'am. He gets the first five minutes or three jokes, whichever comes first. I'm going to make him an even greater speaker...

I remember my mother hanging up the phone with a huge smile on her face. Every other phone call before this ended in tears or her yelling at me. At that moment I vowed to myself that if I was ever a teacher I would call parents to compliment kids.

The next day I walked into English. Mr. D. nodded and I got in front of the room. I promise you all that for the first time in my life I felt good about being in school. I told two of the jokes. And you know what? They didn't boo. And they haven't booed yet. And I haven't sat down yet. I was about to tell the third and then stopped. I looked at Mr. D. and said, "You're up. The third isn't as good as the first two. I need to work on it a bit more." He got right in my ear and said, "Brian, don't ever do that to me again. Now I have to teach longer!" We both laughed and I sat down in my seat. I promise you I never disrupted that man's class again. I didn't let anyone else disrupt it either. In fact, I told people to "shut the F up in his class." Mr. D. had to work with me on that too. But he did because he was a teacher. He didn't teach Math or Science or English or Social Studies or Spanish. He taught kids. All of us.

I have no idea what books we read that year. I have no idea what scores I got on that state exam. I don't remember the name of any other teacher I had that year. But every single day, many years later, I think about a man that helped change my life. I promise you that's what I want to be for my students. Some day somewhere there will be a child that struggled in school but is now a productive member of society. And every day that student will remember me. Your challenging, disruptive, unmotivated students will rarely thank you for never quitting on them. So on their behalf, I want to thank you for being tougher in not giving up on your students than they often are in trying to get you to quit!

References:

Curwin, Mendler, & Mendler, (2009).
Discipline with Dignity 3ʳᵈ Edition. New Challenges New Solutions. Virginia: Association for Supervision and Curriculum Development.

Mendler, Curwin, & Mendler, (2008).
Strategies for Successful Classroom Management. Helping Students Succeed Without Losing Your Dignity or Sanity. California: Corwin Press

Mendler, A. (1997).
Power Struggles. Successful Techniques for Educators. Rochester: Discipline Associates.

Mendler, A. (2007).
More What Do I Do When...? Powerful Strategies to Promote Positive Behavior. Indiana. Solution Tree